"*Soulful Spirituality* is a feast of encouraging wisdom that nourishes soul and spirit. In inviting language, images, and narratives, David Benner describes a way of living that is integrating and inspiring—a hearty blend of psychology, theology, and spirituality for all of us who seek to mature and thrive."

—**Susan S. Phillips**, executive director and professor of sociology and Christianity, New College Berkeley; author, *Candlelight: Illuminating the Art of Spiritual Direction*

"Anything David Benner writes is worth reading, and this is no exception. Read and be fed with real food!"

—**Richard Rohr**, OFM, Center for Action and Contemplation, Albuquerque, New Mexico

"*Soulful Spirituality* embodies the inseparable invitations of the spiritual and human journeys. Dr. Benner's writing is grounded in long years of research and practice at the intersections of human development, psychotherapy, and spiritual direction alongside his own desire to persist in becoming all that God intends. *Soulful Spirituality* stirs the reader's longing for connectedness, fulfillment, aliveness, and wholeness that is uniquely possible through intentional cooperation with God. It invites readers to embrace life as it is and to be open to God in the midst of ordinary/extraordinary reality."

—**Jeannette A. Bakke**, author, *Holy Invitations: Exploring Spiritual Direction*

"*Soulful Spirituality* needs to be read, dialogued with, and then used to overhaul our weak and anemic engagement with the real world. In a culture full of escape-this-world spiritualities on the one hand and narcissistic spiritualities on the other, David Benner says, 'absolutely not!' and then loudly and powerfully links our spirituality to the exciting lifelong task of becoming more fully and deeply human. David's identification of things like toxic spirituality will provide welcome hope to the growing number of people in 'religious recovery' who are on the spiritual and human journey but are simply worn out with the narrow approaches so common today. He has a deep commitment to us as embodied beings and as such helps us attend to an embodied spirituality. He gets at tough concepts like desire, longing, and restlessness, and few have dealt with the issue of ego, its role, and its limits as well as he does in this book. If you are ready to dig in, ready to really change and experience transformation, then by all means get this book. And then buy nine more copies to pass out to friends for a dialogue group!"

—**Ron Martoia**, author, speaker, and founder of *velocityculture.com* and *ttTribe.com*

Books by David G. Benner

Opening to God: Lectio Divina and Life as Prayer (2010)
Desiring God's Will: Aligning Our Hearts with the Heart of God (2005)
The Gift of Being Yourself: The Sacred Call to Self-Discovery (2004)
Surrender to Love: Discovering the Heart of Christian Spirituality (2003)
Strategic Pastoral Counseling: A Short-Term Structured Model, 2nd ed.
   (2003)
Sacred Companions: The Gift of Spiritual Friendship and Direction (2002)
Free at Last: Breaking the Bondage of Guilt and Emotional Wounds (1998)
Care of Souls: Revisioning Christian Nurture and Counsel (1998)
*Money Madness and Financial Freedom: The Psychology of Money Meanings
   and Management* (1996)
Choosing the Gift of Forgiveness: How to Overcome Hurts and Brokenness,
   with Robert Harvey (1996)
Understanding and Facilitating Forgiveness, with Robert Harvey (1996)
Strategic Pastoral Counseling: A Short-Term Structured Model (1992)
Counseling as a Spiritual Process (1991)
Healing Emotional Wounds (1990)
Psychotherapy and the Spiritual Quest (1988)
Therapeutic Love: An Incarnational Interpretation of Counseling (1985)

Books Edited by David G. Benner

*Spiritual Direction and the Care of Souls: A Guide to Christian Approaches
   and Practices*, with Gary Moon (2004)
Baker Encyclopedia of Psychology and Counseling, with Peter Hill (1999)
Christian Perspectives on Human Development, with LeRoy Aden and
   J. Harold Ellens (1992)
*Counseling and the Human Predicament: A Study of Sin, Guilt, and
   Forgiveness*, with LeRoy Aden (1989)
Psychology and Religion (1988)
Psychotherapy in Christian Perspective (1987)
Christian Counseling and Psychotherapy (1987)
Baker Encyclopedia of Psychology (1985)

Soulful
Spirituality

Becoming Fully Alive
and Deeply Human

David G. Benner, PhD

BrazosPress

a division of Baker Publishing Group
Grand Rapids, Michigan

© 2011 by David G. Benner

Published by Brazos Press
a division of Baker Publishing Group
P.O. Box 6287, Grand Rapids, MI 49516-6287
www.brazospress.com

Published in association with Creative Trust Literary Group
5141 Virginia Way, Suite 320, Brentwood, TN 37027
www.creativetrust.com

Printed in the United States of America

Library of Congress Cataloging-in-Publication Data

Benner, David G.
   Soulful spirituality : becoming fully alive and deeply human / David G. Benner.
      p.   cm.
   Includes bibliographical references (p.   ) and index.
   ISBN 978-1-58743-297-2 (pbk.)
   1. Spirituality. 2. Spiritual life—Christianity. I. Title.
  BV4501.3.B4575 2011
  248.4—dc22
                                                               2010030057

In keeping with biblical principles of creation stewardship, Baker Publishing Group advocates the responsible use of our natural resources. As a member of the Green Press Initiative, our company uses recycled paper when possible. The text paper of this book is comprised of 30% post-consumer waste.

11   12   13   14   15   16   17   7   6   5   4   3   2   1

To
Sean and Heather,
who were with me in inner dialogue
as I wrote this book

In memory of
Ruth Penny,
1955–2008,
a dear friend from Auckland, New Zealand,
whose soulful way of living life
helped all who knew her
be more deeply human
and fully alive

If only for once it were still.
If the not quite right and the why this
could be muted, and the neighbor's laughter,
and the static my senses make—
if all of it didn't keep me from coming awake—

Then in one vast thousandfold thought
I could think you up to where thinking ends.

I could possess you,
even for the brevity of a smile,
to offer you
to all that lives,
in gladness.

—Rainer Maria Rilke

Contents

Preface

Metaphors are not just for those of a literary inclination. We all employ metaphors in our speech, but more importantly, we all use those same metaphors to structure our perception and organize our understanding of the world.[1] Our personal metaphors both reflect and shape our experience of ourselves, others, and the world. For this reason I would suggest that metaphors form a deep part of our spirituality.

Take, for example, the life-as-journey metaphor. Although this has become quite popular in spiritual discourse, it is far from the only available metaphor for life. For some people life feels much more like a crapshoot, while for others the metaphor that suggests itself may be that of a battle, a prison, a garden, a roller coaster, a river, or a mission. I am aware that my own fondness for the life-as-journey metaphor reflects a good deal of my own spirituality. It accommodates my restlessness and interminable seeking, and it reflects my tendency to view things in dynamic rather than static terms. More importantly, it fits well with my emphasis on becoming, as well as the closely related theme of transformation. These things made it hard for me to settle into any Christian identity that was based on having arrived or possessing the truth. Being a Christian has been very important to me for most of my life, but it has always meant being a seeker, not simply a finder. My identity as a Christian has had more to do with becoming than with simply being. And what I have wanted to become has been fully alive and deeply human.

Life is a journey of becoming. In Christian terms we might speak of this as becoming our true self in God, becoming like Christ, or possibly becoming our hidden self-in-Christ. In other spiritual traditions this idea has sometimes been presented in terms of becoming enlightened or becoming one with all that is, while in more psychological language it might be framed as becoming increasingly integrated, becoming free, or becoming all we can be. Becoming is an important meeting point of psychology and spirituality. It is an essential characteristic of anything deserving to be called spirituality and is certainly right at the very core of Christian spirituality.

It might strike you as odd, however, to speak of this journey as "becoming fully human." Perhaps you have assumed that we are born fully human or, if not, that this is something that simply requires passage of time. As we shall see, neither of these is true. The fulfillment of our humanity never happens automatically. Nor does it ever occur apart from certain core spiritual ways of living. However, not all spiritual paths—nor even all expressions of Christian spirituality—lead us in this direction. Even as we acknowledge that spirituality plays an indispensable role in this human developmental journey, we must also recognize that it has the potential to make us less, as well as more, authentically human.

It is this contribution of spirituality to the human journey that we will be examining. Our focus will be on ways of living that I will be describing as "soulful." Soulful spirituality is not a spiritual path but a spiritual way of walking the human path. As we shall see, the practices of soulful spirituality are deeply Christian even though none are distinctively Christian. These practices represent spiritual ways of living that support the journey of becoming fully human.

Sometimes our approach to these spiritual ways of living will be from a specifically Christian perspective, while at other times it will be from a broader spiritual perspective—not primarily to demonstrate common ground between Christianity and other spiritual traditions but, more importantly, to help us understand the spiritual dynamics we are considering by placing them in a larger context. At other points we will examine the role of spirituality in the human journey from the perspective of psychology, since, of all the human sciences, it has the most to contribute to our understanding of the inner dimensions of the human journey. But regardless of the vantage point, our focus will be on the process of becoming fully alive and deeply human and the spiritual practices that support this process.

If this is of interest to you, then you have picked up the right book. My primary audience is Christian seekers. This includes those who have been frustrated by what they have found in the church yet who—thankfully—still seek. But it also includes those whose involvement with the church may have been minimal enough to have left them not frustrated but simply unfulfilled, the church seeming to them to be irrelevant to their spiritual quest. Both groups are often surprised to discover how rich a resource authentic Christian spirituality is for the human developmental journey, and I suspect you may also find this to be true.

I have also written this for an even broader group of seekers. Increasingly I encounter people for whom religion was never a significant enough component of their life to provide a meaningful reference point when they first begin to notice their spiritual seeking. Many turn to therapeutic psychology and find in the depth or humanistic psychologies forms of nonreligious spirituality that allow them to start their spiritual journey. Often this will be a journey that is psychologically well grounded but lacking in spiritual self-transcendence. Others draw the form of their spiritual journey from contemporary culture, friends, or personal readings in other spiritual traditions. Once again, I expect that you may be surprised to discover how much a more religious spirituality can contribute to your spiritual practices—in particular, how much Christian spirituality differs from what you had assumed and how richly it could enhance both your human and your spiritual journey.

One final audience has been near the forefront of my mind as I have been writing. People in this group will have a personal interest in spirituality, but they will also have a professional one. They may be students preparing to become teachers, pastors, counselors or psychotherapists, spiritual directors, coaches, mentors, or professionals in any number of Christian ministry fields, or they may already be working in these fields. What they need is a psychologically grounded understanding of spirituality that firmly connects the spiritual journey to the human journey so they can accompany and guide others in their development. Their needs and interests should fit well with those of the other groups for whom I have written.

But having referred repeatedly to the spiritual and human journeys, I should also clearly state that while I understand these developmental pathways to be distinguishable, I also consider them to be inextricably interrelated. Exploring that relationship will be right at the center of what we will undertake in the chapters that follow. While the first two parts of the book present an understanding of how these threads come together—in ways that either compromise or facilitate human development—the third and final part will be much more practical. There our focus will be on spiritual practices that support our becoming fully alive and deeply human.

So let us begin our journey together. I think we will find it to be an experience that will engage our minds and hearts and will have profound implications for our bodies, spirits, and souls. I am convinced it has the potential to help us become more whole, more fully alive, and more deeply human.

PART ONE

The Challenge of Becoming Fully Human

1

The Struggle to Be Fully Alive

As someone who tries to avoid defining myself by who I am not, I am occasionally surprised by my knee-jerk disidentification with religion. Usually this occurs when I hear of yet another appalling act being done in the name of religion—terrorist acts committed, people of other faiths or of no faith murdered, women oppressed, gays and lesbians persecuted, the indigenous members of a society colonized, children sexually abused, the poor patronized, and much more. You are familiar with the litany. All religions appear on this roster of horrifying behaviors, even though many of us are tempted to believe that the really serious problems are primarily associated with faiths other than our own. But I also find myself wanting to distance myself from religion when I meet religious people who are abysmally poor examples of the human species. Too often religion seems to produce or support dogmatic rigidity, prejudice and small mindedness, intolerance, and chronic—even if religiously disguised—levels of anger and hatred. Too often religion seems to contribute to our problems rather than be part of the solution.

My focus in this book will, however, be more on spirituality than religion. Although we will explore the relationship of religion and spirituality in a subsequent chapter where we will examine the potential contribution deep religion can make to spirituality, my primary interest

3

is the role of spirituality in becoming fully human. However, even here it has become clear to me that spirituality does not always add value to life—at least, not to this life, and not in terms of making people more deeply human and whole. Honesty forces me to conclude that the spiritual path can lead to an escape from a robust commitment to reality, the repression or dissociation of sexuality, disconnection from the emotions, alienation from the body, and increasing distance from one's unconscious depths. Too easily, spiritual practices lead to increasing identification with those of one's own religious tribe and an ever-weakening sense of solidarity with all humankind. Too easily, spirituality involves a narcissistic me-and-God relationship that insulates us from, rather than sensitizes us to, the problems of our world. Too easily, it is associated with a focus on beliefs rather than on being. Too easily, it directs us away from life rather than toward a genuinely deeper, fuller, and more vital life. And although these problems are not restricted to religious spiritualities, it seems to me that it is the religious forms of spirituality that are often most vulnerable to these dangers.

Being Spiritual, Being Human

Sometimes I encounter writers and speakers who describe us as human beings on a spiritual journey. I think this is true and have used the same language myself. But I think it is equally true that we are spiritual beings on a human journey. Both journeys are crucial, and each should complement the other. Any religion or spirituality that seeks to make us less than, more than, or other than human is dangerous. Spirituality can and should be in the service of becoming more deeply human. This might surprise you. After all, the human and spiritual journeys are often presented as diametrically opposed to each other, and so it is quite understandable if you have tended to think of the spiritual journey as helping you move beyond the limitations of humanity. During a recent lecture I was giving on these things, a woman sitting in the front row looked puzzled and upset. When I paused for dialogue, she expressed her confusion by saying, "I thought that the more spiritual we become the less human we would be. Isn't being human a sign of spiritual failure? Isn't that why we use being human as an excuse for failures in our best self and our highest way of being?"

Her question illustrates a common and serious misunderstanding of both spirituality and humanity. Humanity is not a disease that needs to be cured or a state of deficiency from which we need to escape. The spiritual journey is not intended to make us into angels, cherubim, seraphim, gods, or some other form of spiritual beings. It is intended to help us become all that we, as humans, can be. How tragic, therefore, that some suggest that the spiritual journey should head in precisely the opposite direction.

Spiritual paths and practices that distance us from what it means to be a human are not good for humans. Quite simply, they are hazardous to our well-being. Rather than making us vital and whole human beings, they leave us impoverished and diminished.

Toxic Spirituality

But how can spiritual paths that we may think of as unquestionably good—for example, our own spiritual path—become so dangerous? There are many routes away from life but only one that points us dependably toward it.

First and most basically, spirituality moves us away from life whenever it distances us from our bodies. The body anchors the spiritual and the mental, grounding perceptions in sensation, feelings in emotion, thoughts in action, defenses in muscles, and beliefs in behavior. Whenever our ties to our body are tenuous, our ties to reality are equally fragile. The body connects us to the truths of our selves, our world, and others. Even our connection to the spiritual realities that many people believe exist beyond materiality occurs in and through our bodies. All knowing is at one level body knowing and all awareness is at one level body awareness. To be human is to be embodied, so any spirituality that fails to take the body seriously necessarily diminishes our humanity.

The role of the body in spirituality is so important that I will devote an entire chapter to it. In chapter 7 we will see that apart from a firm embrace of our bodies, spirituality will always involve an alienation from our emotions, our deepest passions and longings, and our sexuality. Any attempt to gain distance from our bodies will be at the expense of our humanness. The price for this form of avoidance is always high.

One of the ways that we distance our selves from our bodies is by a retreat to the world of thoughts and beliefs. Religious spiritualities encourage this when they reduce the spiritual journey to holding correct theology. In Christianity, the shift from faith as trust to faith as belief was primarily a product of the Enlightenment. The result was a profound shift from the personal/interpersonal to the impersonal. Faith as trust is personal and interpersonal. Trust is always placed in someone or something, and our act of trust is an act of leaning into the object of trust with openness and expectant hopefulness. For Christians, trust in God was slowly degraded, however, into trust in certain thoughts about God. If these thoughts were judged to be true, one was judged to have faith. But the object of faith in this debased expression of faith is, in actuality, thoughts, not God.

I know something about this. For a long time I clutched my ideas about God to my chest, polishing and defending them as if they were the Divine, not simply my pitifully limited construals of Ultimate Mystery. I thought they were truth. Or, more precisely, I thought I had the truth. I did not yet know how to either hold my opinions (including my theology) with humility or be content with living *in* truth as opposed to living in the illusion of *possessing* truth.

(1) Equating faith with beliefs truncates and trivializes spirituality by reducing it to a mental process. Thoughts are, quite simply, a poor substitute for relationship. Some Christians speak much of a personal relationship with God but assume that this is based on holding right beliefs. Is it any wonder that this attempt to reduce Ultimate Mystery to theological propositions so often results in the principal personal relationship being between a person and his or her own thoughts? Cherishing thoughts about God replaces cherishing God; knowing *about* the Divine replaces *knowing* the Divine. Whenever the Wholly Other is thought to be contained in one's beliefs and opinions, divine transcendence is seriously compromised and personal relationship with the Spirit minimized.

(2) Another common way in which the humanizing and transformational capacity for spirituality is trivialized is when it is reduced to practices. Whether it is spinning the Buddhist prayer wheel, whirling as a Sufi dervish, praying the rosary, or reading the Bible, reducing the spiritual life to such practices always reduces the potentially transformational to the ritual.

I think of the many Christians I have met who have been left disillusioned by years of faithful involvement in their church. They may have regularly read their Bibles, faithfully gone to confession, made time for daily personal prayer, attended mass or church services, and served their church in the ways they were asked, yet they found themselves with nothing more than a burden of guilt and frustration. Is it any wonder that they feel Christian spirituality is overrated? Is it any wonder that among those who manage to retain awareness of their underlying spiritual longings, they often fail to even give a thought to Christian spirituality as a framework for that journey?

An interesting story about the late twentieth-century revival of interest in the ancient Christian monastic tradition of Centering Prayer is quite relevant to this point.[1] The three people most responsible for the recovery and popularization of this long-neglected prayer form—Fathers Basil Pennington, Thomas Keating, and William Menninger—were monks at Saint Joseph's Abbey in Spencer, Massachusetts, during the 1970s. They were personally and communally practicing Centering Prayer but had not yet begun to promote it beyond the walls of their monastery. Because of Saint Joseph's location in a valley with a number of other retreat centers, people would often come seeking directions to Barre Center for Buddhist Studies, a meditation center just down the road from the abbey that drew people from around the world. Many of those looking for directions were glad to stop and chat with the monks who quickly discovered that most of these seekers had Christian backgrounds. They told the monks that they were looking for a spiritual path and wanted to learn to meditate. When asked if they had considered the Christian path or any of its meditative traditions, many were invariably surprised, saying that they had never thought of Christianity as a path. Instead, they thought of it as a religion—a set of beliefs and obligations. This led the three monks to devote their lives to making others aware of the rich heritage of Christian contemplative practices. Sadly, the spiritual seekers who sought directions from them share a great deal in common with many contemporary seekers whose spiritual hunger has not been satisfied by the church, leaving them feeling that Christianity is irrelevant to authentic spirituality.

Being a Good Christian Is Not Enough

The reasons Christianity has become irrelevant to the spiritual quests of many people in the West are complex. They begin with the fact that being a good Christian is not the same as being on a spiritual journey. Even more alarming is the fact that being a good Christian does not necessarily make one a good human being. Of course, this is equally true of other religions. I quickly think of people I have known of other faiths whose religious life has made them less than winsome human beings. Regrettably, a commitment to religious beliefs and practices does not always produce a life-enhancing spirituality. Holiness does not automatically translate into wholeness, nor do pietistic practices necessarily lead to an authentically transformational spirituality.

Being a good Christian—or, in language more often used by Roman Catholics, being a good Catholic—often means nothing more than being reasonably regular in attending church services or going to mass or confession. If the bar is raised higher, it might additionally include personally believing the major dogmas of the church. And if it is raised higher still, it might include the religious practices that are particularly valued within the community or tradition—such things as personal prayer or Bible reading, Sabbath keeping, receiving the sacraments, or active involvement in social justice projects. In some Christian traditions it might additionally take the form of a commitment to becoming more Christlike. Unfortunately, all of these things may be nothing more than external conformity to the behavioral norms of a church, denomination, or Christian tradition. All can be present in the absence of an inner transformational journey, and all can be undertaken in ways that fail to deepen one's humanity.

Furthermore, while spiritual practices have a vital role to play in any truly authentic spirituality, the potentially transformational dimension of religious practices is often restricted by the narrow way in which we focus on specific highly prized practices of our path while ignoring the broader dimensions of spiritual living that are common to most spiritual paths. (We will examine these practices in detail in part 3.) All are deeply Christian, but none are distinctively Christian. In fact, as we shall see, most do not even appear to be religious. All, however, are ways of living that anchor the spiritual journey in the human journey. Since it is these dimensions of spiritual living that are most deficient when religion fails to make a person more deeply human and more fully alive, let me briefly identify at this point their negative face—that is, the qualities that are actually present when one is, for example, a good Christian but not on the way to becoming a whole human being.

For example, being a good Christian does not lead to becoming a vital human being if one is living without awareness. Tragically, it is remarkably easy to go through life mindlessly. The default state of consciousness for humans seems to be preoccupation and distraction.

While Christian spiritual practices should awaken us—awakening being a core feature of authentic conversion—often they do not. Unfortunately, we will never be more aware of God or other spiritual realities than we are of our bodies, our emotions, and our experience in the present moment. Living with awareness is a prerequisite to becoming deeply human, but it is not something that comes automatically with being a good Christian.

Good Christians can also easily go through life in a somnambulant fog that blinds them to the enchantment of the world in which they live. We often fail to experience the radical amazement that life should evoke. The most obvious marker of this is boredom. However, most of us become quite adept at warding off this inner sense of deadness and may have no awareness of just how boring we actually find life to be. Compulsive busyness is a particularly good way of defending against boredom. Many people only feel bored on holidays when they find themselves unable to fill the time with enough things to do. But if boredom is the negative face of a spiritual way of living, the positive expression of this life posture is seeing life through eyes of wonder. Spirituality should transform the ordinary into the extraordinary. Religious practices that fail to make us truly alive and deeply human are ones that restrict the wonderful and the extraordinary to the religious realm of life. But this is too small a container, and soon it also proves to be a leaky one. Wonder either fills the world and our experience of it, or it seeps out of life entirely.

Furthermore, being a good Christian does not necessarily make one alert to the spirituality of otherness. It is easy for spiritual practices to help us fit into the subculture of our own religious communities even as they fail to help us experience solidarity with all humans or, even more broadly, with all that is. This failure invariably involves a strong identification with our own tribe and an absence of curiosity about or interest in knowing those who are beyond it. In its darkest expression, this is manifest in terms of prejudicial dismissal of those of other faiths, other ethnic backgrounds, other sexual orientations, or other socioeconomic classes. Rather than being attractive, the otherness of these people is threatening or despised. But limited openness to the otherness of humans always translates into limited encounter with the Ultimate Other—God.

Christian spiritual practices likewise do not necessarily ground a person in the day-to-day realities of life. They should, but this can easily be missed if your focus is otherworldly or, more commonly, if you are preoccupied by a set of spiritual ideals and begin to confuse what is with what you would like to be. The more emphasis a religious tradition or community places on perfection, Christlikeness, or other pietistic ideals, the more difficult it is to be authentically yourself and honestly in touch with the truths of your life. Under such conditions it is alarmingly easy to fake it until you (hopefully) make it, but doing so is always at great cost to your soul.

A busy life of striving to be a good Christian can also very easily sabotage genuine presence to oneself, to others, and to God. Being present requires inner stillness, and good Christians can easily have lives that are so full that there is no space for the cultivation of this stillness. Even the pursuit of spiritual fullness can be an enemy of genuine presence. I know people who are so busy chasing spiritual blessings or insights that they lack the inner space and stillness to be present to anything other than their spiritual desires. Being fully present to God requires that we learn to be truly present to others and to ourselves, and this requires stillness, silence, and solitude— dimensions of spiritual practice that are easily overlooked if you are focusing more on the external dimensions of religious practice.

Finally, it is quite astounding how easily an egocentric, willful life can survive the cultivation of Christian virtues and spiritual practices. The best marker of this is investment in maintaining control. A close second-best sign is the extent to which life is lived with resolve rather than with release and consent. Unfortunately, Christian spiritual practices—or any other spiritual practices—can actually reinforce this natural posture of self-control and self-mastery. When this happens, it seriously limits the fullness of life and depth of humanity that comes from the radically counterintuitive and profoundly Christian practice of surrender.

The Glory of Being Fully Alive

One day a spiritual teacher asked his disciples why God made humans. One of them—an eager young man—answered almost immediately, "That, teacher, is easy. So we can pray." After a brief silence, the teacher asked another question: "Why, then, did God make angels?" The same young man tried again, "Perhaps so that they also could pray." The teacher looked at him and smiled. "The angels," he said, "are perfectly capable of offering prayer to God, but only humans can do what they are uniquely created to do." "What is that?" the eager disciple asked. "What God wants from humans and what only humans can do is become fully human."

Saint Irenaeus, the second-century bishop of Lyons, understood this well. His famous declaration—*Gloria Dei vivens homo*—proclaimed that the glory of God is men and women who are fully alive, fully human. This was a high point in the Christian understanding of the importance of being human, a point so removed from the center of contemporary Christianity that it might almost sound heretical. Could it possibly be true that being human is a good thing, neither a sign of failure or weakness nor a sign of a lack of spirituality? Is it even conceivable that wholeness, not simply holiness, honors God? Is it possible that there could be an alternative to living carefully so as to avoid sin while pursuing the elusive goal of perfection? And could that alternative really be as simple as being and becoming deeply human and fully alive? It does sound too good to be true! It might even make one wonder how Irenaeus was ever declared a saint after making these assertions so central to his teaching.

I have never been motivated to be a saint, but being fully human has been one of my deepest longings for most of my life. Growing up in a theologically conservative Christian denomination that set itself apart from the world left me feeling at one with others who swam in our small faith-pond but desperately wanting to be part of the human race, not just the Christian swimming club. I was struck by the fact that most of the people who seemed most real and authentic were outside that particular club, not within it. I was attracted to their way of being in themselves and in the world. Often they seemed to be at one with themselves and at one with what was. They seemed to be connected to life and able, consequently, to draw their vitality and meaning from life as it actually flowed in and through them. I wanted what they had. I wanted to know how to be fully human, not simply a good Christian.

Perhaps not surprisingly, my sense of vocation grew out of this. Understanding and helping others make the journey toward deep, authentic personhood was the reason I became a clinical psychologist. My focus has never been simply treating psychopathology. Rather, it has been helping people resolve and transcend blocks to becoming all they can be. This is a journey of a lifetime. And, as we shall see, it is a journey that is deeply spiritual.

Facilitating spiritual awareness and response has, therefore, always been a central part of my work in psychotherapy, just as grounding the spiritual journey in the human journey has been a central priority of my work as a spiritual guide. Journeying with others in these boundary places of spirit and soul has convinced me that spirituality is foundational to the human journey. It has made me keenly aware of the dangers of any spirituality that is not rooted in the body and integrally connected to the human developmental journey. But it has also convinced me of the indispensable role of spirituality in becoming fully human and the way in which this occurs when it is anchored in human experience, not simply expressed in beliefs and practices.

The Value of an Accurate Diagnosis

One thing I have often noticed when diagnosing a mental disorder and communicating this to a patient is how liberating and hopeful it can be to hear what might be thought of as bad news. As a young psychologist I used to try to sugarcoat such information in a misguided attempt to make the diagnosis more palatable. Invariably it made things worse. Psychospiritual diagnoses usually do something that medical diagnoses do not always do, namely, provide a way of understanding things that are already present in awareness. Helping people face and understand problems that are being experienced, even if not understood, is the first step to healing. Similarly, the first step toward becoming more than we presently are is always a firm embrace of reality.

There is no sense pretending that being religious—even Christian—automatically makes you a whole, vital, and growing human being. It simply does not. I believe that Christian spirituality can and should lead to all these things. In fact, as I have suggested, I am convinced that becoming fully human—more specifically, becoming the unique and whole human being that I am intended to be—is right at the center of the Christian spiritual journey. But as with anything in the spiritual life, it is essential to start where we actually are, not where we might like to think we are.

Starting Where You Are

If you have read this far, it seems reasonable to assume that there is something within you that is attracted to the possibility of becoming deeply and fully human. We will explore this desire more in the next chapter, but for now, take a few moments to reflect on the things associated with your past or present religious context that might be blocking the fulfillment of this longing. Consider the following as a way of structuring this reflection:

- ✥ I have argued in this chapter that the spiritual life should never make you more than, less than, or anything other than fully human. Do you agree? How do you respond to the assertion of Saint Irenaeus that the glory of God is men and women who are fully alive? Does this fit with what you have been taught or with the emphasis of your spiritual community? If not, in what ways has your spiritual journey compromised your journey to fullness of human personhood?

- ✥ I also suggested that spirituality moves us away from life and compromises our human developmental journey whenever it distances us from our bodies. How integral is your body to your spirituality? Christian spirituality becomes at best irrelevant and at worst damaging to the formation of your humanity when it positions beliefs at the center of the spiritual life. It does so because it makes your spirituality primarily a cognitive matter, not a whole-body, whole-person affair. How disembodied is your spirituality? What important parts of yourself seem to have been left out of your spiritual life?

- ✥ Christian spirituality is also limited in its potential formative influence on your journey to full personhood when it reduces spiritual practices and the spiritual life to a list of superficially religious things. Deep religion penetrates all of life and refuses to accept isolated containment in small overtly religious places. What things did you encounter in this chapter that suggested possibilities for broadening your understanding and practice of the spiritual journey? What have been the implications of holding narrower understandings of spirituality for your journey to this point?

- ✥ Take notice of your desires to be fully and deeply human or to be all you can be. Perhaps you would use quite different language yet still sense that we are talking about the same thing. How would you describe that deep longing? However you have been responding to this longing is an important part of your actual lived spirituality. It may be that you have simply been ignoring it. Or perhaps you have been seeking to respond to it apart from what has seemed like your spiritual life and practices. How would you like to respond to it? How could you make it a more integral part of your intentional spiritual life?

Starting with the challenges that are often part of living out a spiritual life within a religious context can cast religious spirituality in a rather unflattering light. For Christians, it can be a challenge to be a seeker within a culture that may be more oriented to turning seekers into finders. And, as we have seen, it can be a challenge if you are either implicitly or explicitly taught that all you have to do is be a good Christian—however that is defined. But I would not still be a Christian if I did not think that Christian spirituality had truly significant contributions to make to the human developmental journey. I am convinced that it has because I believe that it is a spirituality of becoming, not simply a spirituality of believing or doing, nor even simply of being.

2

Our Restless Hearts

Despite how it is sometimes presented, desire is right at the center of the spiritual life. A sense of obligation may sometimes be enough to keep you going to church, but only desire will keep you open to God and still seeking when your experience in church is filled with frustration and is irrelevant to your deepest spiritual longings. Guilt may be strong enough to motivate religious behavior, but only desire can lead you ahead on the spiritual journey. The absence of desire means the absence of spiritual life. People who are on a spiritual journey are people whose passions point them forward and beyond themselves. As we shall see, the way we respond to our desires is always one of the best available markers of our actual, lived spirituality.

Desire is also indispensable in the journey to full personhood. Willpower may be sufficient for superficial behavioral changes, but only desire is capable of leading you toward deeper authenticity and integrity. No one drifts into such a life without intentionality, commitment, and a persistent desire to become more. No one moves beyond the small, comfortable worldviews and states of consciousness in which we all start life without an abiding desire to grow and become open to that which truly is, not just that with which we feel most comfortable.

Our desires keep us molten, they keep us moving, and they keep us awake—sometimes even in the middle of the night when we would prefer to be asleep! Within each of us is an unquenchable fire, a restlessness that renders us incapable of ever coming to full peace in this life. Our longings will always be larger and more persistent than our satisfactions. They gnaw at the edges of consciousness and are an ever-present reminder that, to paraphrase Plato, "We are fired into life with a madness that comes from the gods and which would have us believe that we can have a great love, perpetuate our own seed, and contemplate the divine."[1] This madness will not let us rest. It propels us forward—eternally seeking, longing, hungering, questing, desiring, and dreaming.

Sometimes it feels like we are searching for the meaning of our existence—or possibly the meaning of our suffering and lack of fulfillment. At other times our quest may seem more related to a search for our place. We long to belong, but we also despair of places of belonging that fail to satisfy our deepest ache. Often it takes the form of a search for a partner or companion. For some, it is experienced as a longing for God, while for others it may take the form of a desire to surrender to something or someone larger than their self.

Regardless of how we understand our persistent restlessness and desiring, we sense that it is of crucial importance. It is a quest that we know is essential to our well-being, sometimes even to our very life. Yet what we find never quite fulfills the longing that drives the quest, and the unquenchable fire leaves us with a constantly restless heart.

Where we seek depends on the way we perceive our longing. Usually we assume that our desire points to something outside ourselves. A story of Nasrudin[2]—the protagonist of much Middle Eastern folklore—reminds us of the folly of this misunderstanding. One night Nasrudin was approaching his house when he realized he had lost his key. He tried to look for it, but the night was so dark he could hardly see anything. He got down on his hands and knees, but it was still too dark to see. Moving back toward a streetlamp, he again got down and began to search the area under the light. A neighbor came by and asked what he was doing. Nasrudin told him he had lost his key, so the neighbor also got down on his hands and knees to search with him. After a while the neighbor asked, "Are you sure you lost the key here?" "No, I didn't lose it here," answered Nasrudin. "I lost it inside my house." "Then why are you looking for it out here?" his bewildered friend asked. "Because," answered Nasrudin, "the light is so much better here."

We are all more like Nasrudin than we want to acknowledge. Most often when we search for our missing key we look outside of ourselves where the light seems good. But the key is inside, in the dark. While what we seek transcends the self, it can only be encountered in the depths of our self. That which we long for is beyond the self, but paradoxically it can only be found within—not, as we shall see, within the ego but within our larger and truer self.

Managing this dark inner source of dis-ease, this cauldron of passionate longings, can be terrifying. The ache from our deep longing often puts whatever peace, coherence, and meaning we have managed to construct for our lives in jeopardy. Our passions may feel dangerous, threatening at times to overwhelm us. But seeking, longing, and desiring are indispensable developmental forces in the realm of spirit and soul. Nothing else is sufficiently potent to keep us moving ahead in the face of frustrations or the numbing comfort of the many way stations where we can easily get stuck.

The Spirituality of Desire

Spirituality is, first and foremost, our response to these deep aches of the soul. Although it may be frightening to trust our desires, they are always fundamentally spiritual. In fact, they are often the most direct access we have to the subtle movement of the Spirit within our own spirits. No matter how mistakenly we interpret these longings, no matter how many times we displace them onto inappropriate objects of desire, they can be trusted because they call us beyond ourselves to our origin, our destiny, and our fulfillment.

The human journey—particularly our spiritual journey—is profoundly shaped by our longings. More often than we expect, we get what we most desire. One way or another, our desires form our spirits and direct our lives. For good or for bad, we are made in the image of what we desire.

My own desire for respect has had a powerful influence on my journey. That influence has, however, generally been negative. While most often I have gotten what I desired, I can now see the price I have paid for my choice. Respect has too often kept other people at a safe distance and forced me to remain content with admiration rather than intimacy. In the same way, a desire for wealth may produce affluence but also easily leads to greed, envy, and dissatisfaction. Similarly, a desire for power saps compassion just as a desire for reputation feeds self-preoccupation. Truly, we are made in the image of what we desire.

When understood superficially, our desires appear to point to our self and our personal gratification. But our deepest desires prove that the universe is not centered on us. They direct us toward that which is beyond our self, to things seemingly just out of reach but toward which our vital energies are oriented. Our desires urge us not to settle for the small, cramped places where we so often live. They pull us toward creative self-expression, expansiveness, and self-actualization. They call us to more-genuine intimacy. They point us toward release from the prison of isolated individuality. They invite us to a place of connection, fulfillment, aliveness, and wholeness.

Our deepest desires call us to a place of both greater height and greater depth. Mystics point out that all desire ultimately leads us to our transcendent Source. Saint Augustine gives us the classic expression of the Christian understanding of this by suggesting that "our soul is restless until it finds rest in thee, O Lord: for thou hast made us for thyself."[3] But because the restlessness occurs in the depths of our soul, our desires also invite us to attend to these depths. They bid us, therefore, to both soar on the winds of spirit and be grounded in the realities of body and soul. They point us toward the self-transcendent but encourage us to remain anchored in the mundane and immanent. They ask us to honor both longing and belonging. They call us to become all we can humanly be.

Managing the Unquenchable Fire

Spirituality, as we have seen, is our response to our inner cauldron of desires. More specifically, one of the central functions of spirituality is the management of the unquenchable fire that is at the core of all living persons. The way we deal with these vital energies will shape our spirituality and will either open us to life or close us off from it. Ronald Rolheiser, a Roman Catholic theologian and popular spiritual author, argues that "spirituality is more about whether or not we can sleep at night than about whether or not we go to church. It is about being integrated or falling apart."[4] He suggests that a saint is someone who can channel these energies in a life-giving way. However, in case this sounds like an easy route to sainthood, it is important to realize just what a challenge it is to integrate our passions. Of the three major ways of managing the inner fire (discussed below), it is by far the most difficult, so it should be no surprise that it is the road less traveled.

But first, let us be clear about what the unquenchable fire actually is. The inextinguishable burning bush that is at the core of our being is our fundamental life energy. Freud called it *eros*. Although this shouldn't be understood simply in sexual terms, it certainly includes the erotic and sexual. But more basically, it is the source of all that vitalizes us. It is, however, primitive and dangerously volatile. It resists channeling. In fact, it resists any form of management. It simply wants gratification—and wants it now. That is why Freud associated it with the id, the most archaic and unregulated dimension of psychic life.

I will refer to the three major ways of dealing with these sources of vital energy as *ego inflation, ego deflation,* and *ego integration.*[5] Beginning with the first two routes—the ones that could be described as broad and much more easily traveled—we will then turn our attention to the narrow and hard path that is such a dependable marker of psychospiritual health.

Ego Inflation

The first way of responding to eros is to pursue the gratification we desire without much or any attempt to channel the energy. This is a life of hedonism and boundlessness—boundless sexuality, boundless creativity, boundless energy, and boundless euphoria. It is a state of inflation. The ego is awash in expansiveness, euphoria, and grandiosity. Of course, such a state can't last forever, so this boundlessness sets us up for an inevitable crash. Living from this place of inflation causes people to burn out fast. Often they die young in a fiery crash. The American actor John Belushi is a good example of this. Dead from a drug overdose at age thirty-three, his was a life of ego inflation—an approach to managing eros that involved a total surrender to drugs, sex, and good times. This was his spirituality, and because of it, in the words of Elton John and Bernie Taupin (originally referring to Marilyn Monroe), his candle burned out long before his legend did. But John Belushi and Marilyn Monroe are far from alone in choosing this way of responding to the fire that is in the belly of us all.

People whose spirituality is organized around managing eros by this strategy of ego inflation seldom come to see psychologists or spiritual directors. When they have come to me for psychotherapy, it has invariably been because they were dragged by their intimates who were being consumed by the immolation that was in process. Most of us can think of friends who don't seem to move on from their adolescent attachments to drugs or alcohol, to sex, or to other high-risk behaviors. Many, of course, move through this in their early twenties. But sadly, others get stuck here. Do not, however, think of this as simply a psychological matter. First and foremost, it expresses their spirituality. It is a spirituality of ego inflation.

Ego Deflation

Another way of responding to the inner fire is to attempt to extinguish it. Many people find their passions and longings to be an unwelcome disruption. These inner stirrings threaten their peace and equanimity because they are associated with pain, frustration, and lack of fulfillment. So they try to shut down the desires. But because it is their basic life energy that they are attempting to shut down, if they did manage to extinguish it they would snuff out their very life. Repressing eros always eliminates the energy we need for living. It lets the air of life escape from the balloon of self. While ego inflation inevitably involves being burned up by passion, ego deflation involves slow death by boredom or depression. Shutting down our passions also leads to alienation from our selves, others, and our world. This is why in depression people turn in upon themselves. Depression is certainly not reducible to a conscious choice to run from eros, but it is one manifestation of this life-destroying posture.

I understand, however, why many people conclude that the safest and easiest way to respond to longings that have often been associated with pain and disappointment is to first try to ignore them and then, noticing that they still have not gone away, to pull in the heavier artillery of repression as a way to eliminate them. I understand why people sometimes give up daring to hope for a partner when their desires lead repeatedly to disappointment. I understand why others eventually give up hope of finding God when churches or Christians place too many obstacles in their path. It is no surprise that many people do everything they can to distance themselves from their desires because of a long history of disappointment and hurt. But when we choose to shut down a longing, we further cut ourselves off from our taproot of vitality, and this always has significant consequences for our psychospiritual well-being. As we shall see, the attempt to shut down awareness of our inner disquiet is the source of all addictions. The price for managing passions by repression is high. Ego deflation is a slower way of killing yourself than ego inflation, but as it extinguishes your vitality it leaves you little more than a shell of a person.

Ego Integration

Healthy spirituality is not simply believing in God or going to church; it is having zest for living and staying glued together. As we move toward an integration of our inner being that is based on channeling our vital energies into self-transcendent causes, we are more likely to avoid fragmentation under stress and our lives will possess passion and vitality.

Life-enhancing spirituality directs our passionate longing and desiring in ways that allow them to be integrated into the fabric of life. However, if our passions are to be integrated they must first be accepted and known. The healthiest expressions of spirituality engage our basic life energy and use it in ways that support the gathering up of all the disparate parts of self. None of us is ever completely integrated. But, as we shall see, spirituality has enormous potential as an integrating force. And it does this by allowing us to embrace rather than repress our deepest longings and passions and then to draw the energy from them to live life with abundance and resilience.

Life-Enhancing Spirituality

Spirituality that enhances life always involves our whole person—body, emotions, sexuality, consciousness, the unconscious, longings and desires, thoughts, the senses and imagination, and much more. For only a lived, holistic spirituality can be transformational, integrative, and capable of helping us become fully alive and deeply human.

I sometimes describe such spirituality as incarnational. While this term is closely associated with Christian theology, its use should not be restricted to Christian spirituality.[6] Most generally, incarnational spirituality is any spirituality that is enfleshed and lived, not simply believed or practiced. It is a spirituality that orients us toward life as it is lived here and now, in our embodied existence. The truth is that we do not need to dissociate from our bodies or distance ourselves from the realities of life in order to live spiritually. Spirituality need not be an escape from anything. It can instead be the completion and integration of every aspect of life.

Because I have focused so much up to this point on the challenges of developing a healthy, life-enhancing spirituality, let me offer here a brief sketch of the unique potential that spirituality holds for the human journey.

- It can connect us to the realities of our life, grounding us in the places where we actually live rather than the illusory castles in the sky where we might prefer to live.
- It can allow us to feel equally at home and spiritually grounded in both the mundane details of everyday existence and the mountaintop experiences of spiritual ecstasy.
- It can release us from the prison of our mind and bring us back to our senses.
- It can awaken us to our life and help us fully live it rather than merely exist within it.
- It can connect us to the truths of our depths that are normally beyond awareness.
- It can introduce us to new ways of being at peace with our self as we learn to welcome that which might be unchosen and even undesired but that is, nonetheless, part of our reality.
- It can connect us to others in ways that are more respectful and honoring, allowing us to be more at peace with others and with the world.
- It can free us from the small life of the ego and introduce us to our place in relation to the self-transcendent.
- It can help us remain open to mystery in our world and in our life.
- It can allow life itself to become meaningful.
- It can help us relearn wonder and awe and soften our grasp on reason and control.
- It can help us find joyous involvement in a worthy vision that transcends our ego-self and that serves our world and its inhabitants.
- It can increase the possibility of our noticing the brushes with the Wholly Other that grace our life.

- And finally, it can help us say yes to life (or to God) as we open ourselves in trust and surrender.

These dynamics of healthy spirituality will be our focus in parts 2 and 3. They leave us, however, with one important question that we must address in at least a preliminary way in this chapter: what is spirituality?

What Is Spirituality?

In the last several decades Western culture, particularly in North America, has been so flooded with books, magazines, television shows, and other media related to spirituality that most people are quite familiar with the concept. However, the understanding of spirituality that is part of this familiarity usually contains serious misunderstanding and much confusion.

One of the most frequent misunderstandings is the equation of spirituality and religion. Many people assume that spirituality is a euphemism for religion. I recall an interesting experience a few years ago when I interviewed for a faculty appointment in a medical school. The dean had scanned my vita and, seeing the large number of publications that had to do with spirituality, first asked if I had been a priest before I became a clinical psychologist. I told her I had not. She then asked whether I had always wanted to be a priest. I told her I had never even considered the possibility. This obviously surprised her because of her conflation of spirituality and religion, but getting this out of the way did let us get on with the interview.

However, while many people assume a close association between spirituality and religion, large numbers of people claim to be spiritual but not religious. Many of those who are self-consciously on a spiritual journey feel enough discomfort with religion that they distance themselves from at least its institutional expressions. Often these people have concluded that there is no genuine spiritual path associated with their religion of upbringing. I have heard this from Jews, Christians, and Muslims who have abandoned their own religious heritage to find what seemed to them an authentic spiritual path. Invariably, what they were abandoning were soulless versions of spirituality as they sought something that was more genuinely life giving.

What these people often do, of course, is follow the well-worn path to the East. Adventurers have long felt the call to the West, but spiritual seekers have usually headed to the East. Buddhism, Hinduism, Taoism, and other Eastern religions have long attracted followers from the West. This journey is often valuable in the spiritual growth of seekers since a change of spiritual context can be helpful in allowing us to see what we missed in our own more familiar life space. The wisest of the spiritual guides of the East have recognized this and have typically encouraged these seekers to reconnect with their own religious heritages. Thich Nhat Hanh, the Vietnamese monk and Zen master who has had such a large following in the West, is a good example of this, encouraging those who come to him to recognize that in order to learn deeply from the Eastern traditions they must be truly open to and engaged with their own. "For dialogue to be fruitful," he argues, "we need to live deeply our own tradition and, at the same time, listen deeply to others. Through the practice of deep looking and deep listening, we become free, able to see the beauty and values in our own and others' tradition."[7]

Properly understood, spirituality is a dimension of the life of all people, not merely those of a religious persuasion or a particular personality type. It is no more possible for a person to not be a spiritual being than it is to not be an embodied being. Spirituality is a fundamental part of human personhood. Everyone has a spirituality, whether they think of themselves as spiritual or not. The difference between people is how attentive they are to spiritual yearnings, how they respond to these yearnings, and whether or not their response is life giving.

Spirituality is our way of living in relation to that which is beyond the self. Because it is a way of living, it is not something that can ever be reduced to beliefs or practices. Our spirituality, which is much more than what we think or do, shapes how we orient our life in relation to that which is transcendent to our self. Regardless of how we choose to do this—and in upcoming chapters we will explore some of the many possibilities—the result will be our spirituality. It will guide our response to our deepest longings, channel our vitality, and provide the framework within which we make sense of our life. It will also be the reference point around which our life and experience are integrated.

While everyone has a spirituality, our actual spirituality—that is, the way we live our life in relation to that which is beyond our individual self—is often surprisingly different from what we think it is. There are a great many ways that we can organize our life around a relationship with something that is transcendent to our self. I think, for example, of people I know for whom being Christian forms an important part of their identity and who are quite religiously active. However, their spirituality is not primarily Christian. This doesn't mean that it is bad or that it is anti-Christian; it simply means that it may not be what they think it is. Their Christian faith may not organize how they live in relation to that which is transcendent to (or beyond) them. Their functional spirituality—that which actually organizes their lives and channels their vitality—might be something quite different.

Take, for example, people who live with what I would call a spirituality of music. It is not simply that these people like music, nor that they may earn a living by making music. It is more a matter of music making their life worthwhile. It is their fundamental life passion. Music has the power to transport them somewhere beyond themselves; consequently, they place a supreme value on music. Sometimes they may use the language of spirituality to refer to their experience with music. Often, however, they will simply live that spirituality as a deep, unnamed way of anchoring themselves in something profoundly self-transcendent. Regardless of whether they identify themselves as Christian or New Age or nonspiritual, their actual, functional spirituality might be primarily a spirituality of music.

We will look at other examples of the difference between an assumed spirituality and the actual, functional spirituality in the next chapter. The point I want to make here is simply that our actual spirituality will always be something profoundly personal. Sometimes it is so deeply personal that it is quite hidden from us. Other times we don't see it or recognize it for what it is because we are confusing it with religion, ethnicity, or culture. But it will always be present, regardless of whether we think of ourselves as spiritual.

Assessing Your Actual Spirituality

Take a few moments to consider the following as a way to begin discovering your own actual—not simply your assumed—spirituality:

+ In this chapter I gave the broad contours of an understanding of spirituality that will be further developed as we proceed. That starting framework was built around the management of our basic life energy and our way of relating to that which is transcendent to us. How do you understand spirituality—not Christian spirituality or some other specific spirituality, but spirituality in general? Take a few moments to write out a definition that works for you at this point in time, and then note how it evolves as you continue to read through the rest of the book.

✢ Now reflect on your life as if you were someone other than yourself who was observing you. In what way(s) is your life oriented around that which is beyond your individual self? How does this relate to your deepest passions and longings? And how does it help make your life meaningful?

✢ What have been your deepest and most persistent longings? How have you responded to them? How have you generally managed your deep passions and life energy?

✢ Finally, to what extent does your actual spirituality support a deepening of your humanity, your creativity, and your zest for living a full and vital life? What aspects of your spirituality lead you away from your body, your sexuality, your emotions, or your experience?

If spirituality at its best should be a way of living life that helps us become more deeply human, we need to think a bit more carefully about just what it means to be human. Once we do so, we will then be in a position to better understand the journey of becoming fully human. We turn to these things in the next chapter.

3

Understanding Our Humanity

I have not always seen it this way, but at this stage of my life I count being human my second-greatest gift. The first is life itself.

These two gifts are, of course, closely connected. As a human, I am unable to know life as a rock, or as a flower, a bird, or a god. I can, however, know life as a human being. Being human is the only way I can truly engage with life. Being fully human is, therefore, profoundly important if I want to be fully alive.

But you may wonder if I am making too much of something we can safely take for granted. Perhaps, you might suggest, being human is natural—the default option for beings that are capable of being nothing else. However, while there is truth in the fact that we are not capable of being anything other than human, we are alarmingly capable of being less than fully human. Witness the atrocities we have perpetrated on others whose humanity we have denied because they held beliefs that were different from ours—or because their skin was darker than ours, or their otherness too uncomfortable for us. Or think of how we so easily slip into a kind of oblivion and live like subhuman automatons, devoid of awareness and failing to exercise our fundamental human capacity for choice and action.

Being fully alive, fully awake, and fully human are far from normal or automatic occurrences. But before we examine more closely why

27

this is and what we can do about it, we should first consider the more basic question of what it means to be human. Our answer to this will lay the foundation for our discussion of what it means to live in a manner that is both deeply spiritual and deeply human.

What Makes Us Human?

Shortly before his death, Henri Nouwen was invited to deliver a special lecture at a university where I was teaching. His years as a professor at Notre Dame, Yale, and Harvard universities made his scholarly credentials impeccable. However, his life since leaving the academy suggested that this might be no ordinary academic lecture. He had spent those years in Toronto in the L'Arche community of Daybreak—a community made up of developmentally disabled persons and a few helpers. He came onto the stage with several of the people he lived with, informing his audience that since moving to Daybreak he never traveled alone. He then invited his Daybreak friends to interrupt him at any point if they had something they wanted to say. Several of them did so—several times. It was, indeed, no ordinary academic lecture!

The topic of his talk was "What makes us human?" This, he said, had become a central question for him since leaving the world of the Ivy League universities and moving into L'Arche. He began by reviewing the standard list of things suggested by anthropologists and evolutionary psychologists as distinctive to humans—such things as self-awareness, speech and symbolic cognition, conscience, the ability to contemplate our origins and our future, and the capacity to imagine. These, he noted, were all the product of the mind, and consequently, it was the mind that both the academy and the world had come to assume was the centerpiece of our humanity. But living with the developmentally disabled had forced him to rethink this. If the mind was primary in what makes us human, those who were intellectually deficient must be seen as less than fully human. However, life with these wonderful people taught him that they were far from subhuman. From them he learned that it was not the mind but the heart that makes us most fundamentally human.

The assumption that thinking is at the core of what makes us distinctively human is easy to understand since thinking is so present in our experience. Thoughts form the almost constant background noise of ordinary consciousness. If you doubt this, take a moment for a little experiment. Pay attention to the stream of thoughts, memories, sensations, and awareness that passes through your mind over the next thirty seconds. One thought leads to the next, and within a flash, to something else, and then to something new yet again. For example, you might first notice that you are thinking about thinking. Then, observing some peripheral movement, you look to the side and see a bird fly past the window. Then you notice that you are aware of a slight headache, which leads immediately to remembering that you have not yet had breakfast, followed by a mental image of a plate of toast and a cup of coffee. Suddenly you might remember a task you must do. And so it goes, on and on. One thought leads to another, one awareness to another. Buddhists call this the monkey mind because, just as the monkey jumps from tree to tree, so too our thoughts follow a chain of invisible associations that result in ceaseless inner restlessness. In the words of T. S. Eliot,

> Endless invention, endless experiment,
> Brings knowledge of motion, but not of stillness;
> Knowledge of speech, but not of silence;
> Knowledge of words, and ignorance of The Word.[1]

Nevertheless, even though our thoughts are fickle, we strongly identify with them. Often they seem to be the most personal things we possess, and in many ways, they are. My thoughts are mine. I can hold them in secret or display them in public ways that present me to best advantage. They are, however, *my* thoughts. I may not be able to control them, but I do get used to their constant presence and this further strengthens my identification with them. Over time, I also learn that I can use my thoughts to bring comfort when I hurt, coherence when I am confused, and order when I feel threatened by chaos. They are the adult's version of the infant's soother or pacifier—a private and very personal comforter that is always available to do its job of bolstering identity, security, meaning, and self-esteem.

Noting this pervasiveness of thought led Descartes to his famous conclusion about human existence: "I think, therefore I am." But is thinking really the essence of who I am? Am I my thoughts? Do I remain human even in the absence of thought? How important is thinking to the fulfillment of my humanity? Might there be something even more fundamental to my being a human person?

Dust and Breath

The Judeo-Christian creation story gives us a helpful way of approaching this important question. The Bible describes the creation of the first human in the following words: "Yahweh God fashioned man of dust from the soil. Then he breathed into his nostrils a breath of life, and thus man became a living being" (Gen. 2:7).

Dust is the stuff of the earth. Humans are creatures of the earth and inextricably connected to the material world. This is vitally important, particularly for anyone interested in spirituality. Whatever spirituality is, it should not be something that pulls us away from the material world. To be human is to have a fundamental attachment to the earth. The spiritualities of the world's indigenous peoples have long recognized this and given it an important place in their practices, as do some of the Eastern spiritualities (for example, Taoism). Western religious spiritualities have been much slower in recognizing the importance of this ecological dimension of our connectedness to that which is beyond us.

Notice what animates this handful of dust—the divine breath. Divine breath transforms inanimate dust into a living, human person. Christians understand this breath as God's Spirit—the English word *spirit* comes from the Latin *spiritus*, meaning "breath." For Christians, our animation comes from the inner presence of the Spirit of God. Creation stories from other religious traditions present slight variations on this Judeo-Christian account. The Qur'an describes Allah's creation of Adam in the following words: "We created man from sounding clay, from mud molded into shape."[2] Mud and clay are, of course, both more substantial than dust, which, in the Christian account, points to the internal spaciousness that exists even in our human physicality. This lightness of being is also captured in the sacred Taoist text *T'ai Shang Ch'ing-ching Ching* (*Cultivating Stillness*), which states that "humans are created from the descent of heavenly breath and the ascent of earthly vapor."[3]

Humans are connected, therefore, to both heaven and earth. Life is to be lived with awareness of these two reference points for our identity and meaning. For the development of full-orbed personhood we must be anchored in the material realities of our physical environment but also connected to the ultimate horizon that Paul Tillich called the ground of our being. Our relationship with both is vital to becoming fully human.

Holding dust and breath together is not easy. Too much breath or a good gust of wind and the dust blows away. Dust is so impermanent that we might be tempted to solidify it with some water and then let it bake in the sun before we expose it to a breeze. Or we might be tempted to focus on the breath and ignore the dust, downplaying the physicality of humans and emphasizing only their spiritual nature. Honoring both as constituent dimensions of being human requires living in the tension that exists between dust and breath. Life must be lived in a way that honors both material and spiritual realities if we are to find our place and fulfillment as human beings. We will never find fullness of life in either of these to the exclusion of the other.

Of course, the easiest horizon to lose sight of is the one that is immaterial and is, therefore, unknowable to the senses. This has been the story of modernity in the West, the result being the reduction of humans to their bodies and the desacralization of the world. The central place of divine breath in the various creation stories points us to this easily overlooked horizon.

Lightness and Mystery

I mentioned the lightness of being that is ours as creatures of dust and breath, but I want to say more about this because it is very important to an understanding of spirituality. Spirit invites us to live in the place of airy spaciousness and lightness of being that is our origin and destiny. There is something fundamentally wrong with a spiritual journey that makes you more substantial. Creatures of dust and breath are more like works of installation art than something in a permanent exhibition. Ego wants permanence and importance and is disdainful of anything that is here today, gone tomorrow. But from dust we come and to dust we shall return—everything passing, nothing even to be remembered (Eccles. 1:11; 3:20).

The Christian mystic Hildegard von Bingen described herself as being a feather on the breath of God. Such lightness comes only with emptiness, both being fundamentally important parts of the spiritual life. Buddhists speak of the dangers of spiritual materialism, referring to a spirituality of acquisitiveness and possessiveness. For some the spiritual journey becomes nothing more than acquiring insights, understandings, and experiences. For others it is mastering spiritual practices or acquiring spiritual proficiencies. Sadly, however, these things are all spiritual possessions, and—like any possession—they easily begin to possess us. Approaching the spiritual life with a need for understanding or a desire for experiences of ecstasy or blessing will quickly produce a spirituality of heaviness, not lightness. A spirituality of lightness is a spirituality of nonattachment in which we resist the temptation to cling to our understanding, our explanations, our experiences, our habits and disciplines, and our beliefs. Real faith is rooted in being willing to acknowledge our fundamental inability to know much about ultimate things. It contents itself with what the Christian mystics have described as living in a cloud of unknowing— and living in that misty place with lightness of being.

Authentic spirituality grows out of emptiness, not fullness. Often we are too full to know our deep hunger and too substantial to experience our actual lightness of being. I know that has been true for me. I have often been too full of myself—my understandings, my opinions, my needs, my projects and priorities, even my spiritual journey. Preoccupations such as these always weigh us down and close us off to the transcendent.

Spirituality that supports the human journey will always be rooted in a life that is open to the vitalizing and transformative breath of the Spirit and to the mysteries of life and faith. It does not lose sight of the fact that we never really "get" spiritual matters; rather, they "get" us. It appreciates that, in the words of Thomas Moore, "At best we can never be more than approximately correct when we speak about spiritual matters. The part that remains unknown and unspoken gives our words and ideas the emptiness they require."[4] Authentic spirituality leaves room for mystery and thus helps us preserve the lightness of being that is our heritage as creatures of dust and breath.

The Spirituality of Being and Becoming

Authentic spirituality is also a spirituality of becoming. Being itself contains this important dynamic of becoming. The roots of the English-language verb *to be* make this clear. The Sanskrit form of this verb is *bhu*. Literally translated this means "to grow into being" or "to become." Becoming is a foundational part of being, particularly of human being. To be human is to possess a vital drive to become—to relentlessly push toward the goal of fulfilling our self, of becoming all we can be. The quest to flourish is deeply embedded in being human.

From the perspective of Islam, Judaism, and Christianity, this quest is rooted in the *imago Dei*. The human quest to become is a spiritual reflection of our participation in the life of the Spirit.

Because authentic spirituality participates in life rather than positioning itself either against or outside the flow of life, it is endlessly evolving and changing. While change sometimes may be resisted, it should be welcomed as the very heartbeat of life—the sure sign that life still pulses through the world, inviting not just our own personal growth but human and cosmic evolution. From a theistic perspective, change is the sign that God remains present and active, holding and sustaining all things in the Divine Being and moving all of life forward toward actualization and completion. Spirituality that supports the human journey will always involve saying yes to this flow and consenting to participate in this great journey of becoming.

Becoming balances doing and being. Spiritual teachers sometimes put too much distance between doing and being, as if one could ever be without any doing, or do without any being. The point they are usually trying to make when they assert the priority of being over doing is that all human doing should emerge out of our more basic being. We are, after all, human beings, not human doings. One way to keep doing and being in equilibrium is to keep the horizon of becoming always in sight. The person who is no longer in a process of becoming is a person who has lost something fundamental to full-fledged humanity. Perhaps this state of nonbecoming is what Christian theology refers to as hell—something that for too many people is a present reality devoid of becoming and devoid of vitality.

An embrace of becoming all that we can be is a deeply spiritual way of living. It orients us to that which is larger and beyond our individual selves, channeling our vitality and making life meaningful. It is a spirituality of growth and the fulfillment of our potentialities.

Louise was in her early forties when she contacted me and asked for help with this journey of becoming. She was a successful but unhappy psychiatrist who felt seriously alienated from the culture of her profession. Initially attracted to psychiatry because of its promise of being a holistic way of working with people, she instead found herself reducing her patients to neuropsychological deficits that could then be treated with drugs. More serious than not simply liking what she was doing, she said that her training and work had made her a smaller person. This she felt was an unacceptably high price to pay, and she was ready, therefore, to leave medicine and pursue something else. Her career transition was not, however, what she wanted to discuss with me. What she wanted from me was help in becoming more whole.

We began by exploring her sense of being less than whole. She said that the best way she could describe it was in terms of the feeling of not being at one within her self or at one with the world. Something was out of alignment; she felt incomplete. The lack of completion could not be explained in terms of her life circumstances since she had all the things that were normally associated with fulfillment—a loving husband and two children, a nice home, good friends, sufficient income to do most things she could ever want to do, and much more. But in spite of these things, she felt that she had compromised on her life. She felt that she could be more—not do more, but be more. She said that if she were a religious person she might describe her problem as spiritual. But, she said, she wasn't even sure if she knew what this word meant. What she did know was a longing to expand her boundaries, to become deeper, higher, and wider. She wanted a more expansive ground beneath her feet and a larger horizon in front of her. And, she told me, her longing for these things was as strong as any longing she had ever experienced in her life. It came with a sense of urgency—almost crisis. She felt certain that if she did not take this longing seriously, something within her would die.

Over the course of our work together, Louise began to find the larger horizons and firmer footing she was seeking. Her sense of alignment with the world and within herself also increased. Central to both of these shifts was the change in her identity as she slowly moved from identification with her work, accomplishments, and possessions to identification with humans in general and life itself. She did, in fact, leave medicine and was, when I last heard from her, finishing a PhD in religious studies. But the important changes that she made were internal, not external. They were spiritual because they had to do with how she lived her life in relationship to self-transcendent realities and callings—in her case, the call to become all she could be.

Becoming Fully Human

Confucian philosophy and developmental psychology share at least two important convictions about being human. Both believe that humans are never born fully human and that the mere passage of time is insufficient in itself to ensure the development of full human personhood.

Newborns may bear the potential for mature personhood, but they do not show any of the characteristics that humanistic psychologists—the psychologists most concerned with psychological maturity and human actualization—have identified. Markers of fully actualized humanity include such things as a well-developed capacity for non-possessive love, being grounded in reality and alive in the present moment, a personal philosophy that makes life meaningful, the capacity for forgiveness and letting go, inner freedom of choice and response, creativity, respect for others, the capacity for reflection on experience, and an identification with all humans, not simply those with whom one most easily identifies. Many other things could be added to this list, but even in this partial form it shows the magnitude of the task of achieving full-orbed personhood.

Another way of describing mature personhood is in terms of advances on the various lines of human development. We all differ on dimensions of life such as cognition, moral reasoning, and emotional functioning. Similarly, we differ in terms of the maturity of our ego development, the breadth and openness of our worldview, our capacity for love, and our ability to adopt perspectives other than our own. Underlying all of these are fundamental differences in the development of consciousness itself—the great evolving ocean of awareness on which all phenomena and experiences arise. But while these competencies are all markers of the fully actualized human, none exist at birth and none are acquired simply by the passage of time.

Time is necessary but not sufficient in the human journey. Many other things are also necessary—including adequate love and emotional support, a healthy balance between gratification and frustration, courage, honesty, an openness to experience, a commitment to growth, freedom from both external and internal restrictions, and much more.[5] Confucian thought gives particular emphasis to the essential role of consciously making a decision to become all one can be. According to the *Li Chi*, the classic Confucian guide to becoming fully human, there must be a turning point in life when the maturing individual recognizes that simply *being* a human is not sufficient to *becoming* fully human.[6] Out of this awareness the person must then resolve to become all she or he can be. Confucians call this, and the subsequent journey, the great learning.

Integral psychology—a holistic approach that makes its central concern the evolution of human consciousness—places a similar emphasis on the intentional nature of the journey to full human personhood. Ken Wilber argues that life practices that attend to body, mind, and spirit are essential for significant advances on any of the lines of inner development.[7] Some growth comes from openness to life experience, but expansion of consciousness—which, in his view, fuels and supports all other development—requires conscious choice and commitment to our becoming all we can be.

Christian teaching has not always been as clear as these other approaches have been about the importance of becoming human. Sometimes it has seemed to support a spirituality of escape from the human condition, particularly from our bodies, emotions, and sexuality. In this, it has failed to take seriously the Bible's clear and strong affirmations of the goodness of the material world in general and of humanity in particular. Salvation as escape from humanity is sub-Christian. Saint Irenaeus got it right when he declared that the glory of God is humans fully alive!

This was clearly the message of Jesus. Contrasting himself with those who come to steal or destroy life, he declared that the reason he came to earth was to bring abundant life and to help people live that life to the full (John 10:10). Sometimes—for example, during his encounter with the Samaritan woman at the well—he described this full life as eternal (John 4:14). This word *eternal* is a bit misleading here as it suggests something that would be experienced after death—some sort of immortality. This is not what Jesus was offering. The life that he offered is the life of the Eternal One. It is the life of God, welling up within as a spring of living water.

The real challenge of humanity is more a matter of becoming than simply being. It is about drawing deeply from this inner spring of living water that vitalizes and allows us to become fully human. It is about living in the present, fully awake and ready to engage with life, with the people around us, and with the world. It is about choosing life.

Choosing Life

Choosing life is not only foundational to deep spirituality in general terms; it is also a fundamental part of Judeo-Christian spirituality. Recall the last words of Moses to the children of Israel just before he died (Deut. 30:15–20). He described two ways of living—a way of life and a way of death. Choosing life, he told them, was choosing God. Equally true, choosing God is choosing life. Jews remind themselves of this every time they offer a toast. *L'Chaim* means "to life." Not only is life worth drinking to, but it is worth being lived as an ongoing celebration. Doing so is a way of honoring God because, as Saint Irenaeus reminds us, God is glorified when we are fully alive.

Take a few moments to reflect on this understanding of spirituality and on the state of your own being and becoming fully human.

- ✣ What role do you think openness to life should play in spirituality? What part does choosing life actually play in your own spirituality? How does it fit with the way spirituality is understood and practiced within your tradition and community?

- ✣ How much lightness of being do you experience? What would it be like to be a feather on the breath of God? In this chapter I have argued that authentic spirituality grows out of emptiness, not fullness. What things weigh you down and leave you too full to know the emptiness of vitalizing spiritual longings?

- ✣ I have also suggested that becoming fully human demands choice and intentionality. Much more than a one-time decision, it is a spiritual way of living that is characterized by a commitment to becoming, not simply to being. What have you allowed to get in the way of being fully alive and becoming all you can be?

In his book *Becoming Human,* Jean Vanier writes that the lifelong journey of all humans involves growth in freedom, an opening up of our hearts to others, stepping out from behind the walls of our fears and prejudice and discovering our common humanity.[8] This is what Henri Nouwen had in mind when he suggested that the heart is more basic to humanity than the mind. And I am convinced that spirituality is integral to this journey toward a deep and full humanity.

Spirit and soul both have an important role to play on the path to becoming fully human. Each of these metaphoric concepts points to one dimension of our inner life. We turn now to the way in which they come together in a spiritual life that is grounded in human becoming.

PART TWO

The Path to
Becoming Fully Human

4

Living with Spirit and Soul

I t is frustratingly clear to those who seek to eliminate mystery from life that spirit and soul bring us right up to the edge of some of the most profound mysteries of our existence. Words seem to fail when we move into this place where dust is animated by the divine breath. Everything is alive and moving—charged with energy. It is dynamic, organic. It is impossible, therefore, to treat it as something inert and to place it beneath a microscope of analysis. This means that it is somewhat misleading to speak of understanding spirit and soul. Instead we should probably speak of honoring them, living them, or learning from them. However, since the terms are ambiguous, if I am to use them it is important that I say more about what I mean by them.

Words like *spirit* and *soul* obviously come to us with a good deal of baggage. In fact, some argue that these concepts are so contaminated by their premodern philosophical and theological roots that they are Trojan horses that threaten to drag us back into the bondage of religious superstition. Others might be inclined to borrow the British philosopher Gilbert Ryle's suggestion that such language simply puts the ghost back into the human machine[1]—a machine that science, we are told, has shown can run just fine without such spectral oversight!

Although I do not agree with these conclusions, I do appreciate the metaphors. They illustrate the power of imaginative and poetic language. You do not have to be familiar with the history of the Trojan wars or have had personal experience with the software viruses called "Trojan Horses" for the words to conjure up associations of treachery and danger—something appearing to be benign that is actually malevolent. Describing nonscientific concepts about the inner life of persons as a ghost in the machine offers us another example of such language. With a couple of words you get something much richer than a definition; you get a network of inner associations that flesh out the bare-bones meaning of the words by opening up richer possibilities of understanding.

My use of the concepts of spirit and soul involves this sort of imaginative language. In fact, only by means of such language can we really talk about things like spirit and soul at all because, as James Hillman points out, they are not things but viewpoints, more a perspective than a substance.[2] This means that we must be careful to avoid getting too literal in discussing them. We must not treat them more concretely than they are. And we must be content with images and metaphors as ways of describing them.

The terms *spirit* and *soul* refer to ways of living, not to parts of self. Humans are an organic whole, not a collection of parts. We do not possess a soul, but we are soul. Similarly, we do not possess a spirit or even a body; we are spirit and we are body. Spirit and soul are ways of speaking about the whole person while drawing attention to dimensions of human existence that are important but easily overlooked.

Both spirit and soul call us to a journey. Although, as we will see in what follows, each seems to take us in a slightly different direction, a response to one connects us to and gives opportunity for a response to the other. I am convinced that both journeys enrich and deepen the basic human journey and allow us to become more fully alive and deeply human. I also believe that neither journey taken on its own can do this. A spiritual journey that is not attentive to the call of soul leaves us ungrounded in some fundamental way, and a journey of soulfulness that is not responsive to the call of spirit leaves us self-encapsulated. We are all prone to both of these imbalances, although one or the other will usually predominate at any given point in our journey.

Notions of spirit and soul do not reintroduce a ghost to the human machine. Rather, they show us the total inadequacy of viewing humans as machines. Of course, sometimes we live in a machine-like manner. This is, however, human life in its most impoverished form—lacking in vitality and depth, lacking in spirit and soul, lacking humanity.

What value, then, do these concepts add to our understanding of persons? No single representation of either does justice. To understand them, we must notice them in our peripheral vision rather than look at them directly. There, we may catch fleeting glimpses of spirit and soul, each glimpse adding to the growing sense of what these basic dynamics of human life represent.

Spirit as Fire in the Belly

What registers in our senses when we catch a glance of spirit often involves sparkle—some combination of light and movement. Spirit is dynamic, energizing, vitalizing, and enriching. Like fire and wind, spirit ignites, moves, and animates. It gives us the energy to live life to the full. Think of what it means to speak of someone having their spirit broken or losing their spirit. What we usually mean by this is that such a person has lost their zest for living. They might feel deflated or even depressed. They might have lost their spark or their energy. Talk about team spirit suggests something similar, reinforcing this equation of spirit with a sense of enthusiasm, expansiveness, and vitality.

Without spirit, we have no life. The Gospels describe Jesus as giving up his spirit and dying. To lose your spirit is to be on a deathwatch. Unless you can recover your spirit, you will die because spirit is life. Spirit is the fire in the belly that we need if we are to live as humans, not machines. It is the vital life energy that Freud called the life instinct. Spirit kindles passions that make life worth living. Spirit animates, sustains, and gives purpose and direction to life.

We have already noted the role of spirituality in the management of this fire in our belly. First and foremost, our spirituality is what we do with our vital life force. It is how we channel our desires and shape our actions. Tragically, too often spirituality shuts down this fire in the belly. Because my own spirituality dampened my passions at an early stage of my journey, I am keenly attentive to passions when I talk with people. In psychotherapeutic or spiritual guidance dialogue, if I fail to notice passion, I always ask about it. Far too often people tell me that they are not passionate about anything. Without knowing anything else about such a person's spirituality, I immediately know that it is soulless. It does not bring them life.

Our spirituality should give us the energy that we need to engage with life. Any spirituality that is life-giving will also put us in touch with our deepest longings and will move us into the world in a way that makes our life meaningful. Spirit is the underlying source of our generativity. It drives us toward fullness, wholeness, and integration. It has many dimensions, and we will be exploring these throughout the remainder of this book. None of these can happen, however, unless we channel our passions and vital energies in a healthy way. When this happens, spirituality is in the service of the integration of personhood.

An unhealthy spirituality will always first fail in this basic task of helping us manage the fire in our belly. In some cases, it distances us from our body, emotions, and deepest longings. In others, it feeds the grandiosity and expansiveness that accompanies unchanneled vital energies and leads to ego disintegration. Whether through repression or disintegration, unhealthy spirituality always fragments rather than makes us whole.

Soul as the Womb of Experience

If spirit is the fire in our bellies, we immediately see the need for something that can help us contain this fire, sometimes even cool it down. We need a womb of safety and containment, and this is what soul offers. We are forever in a forge—our spirits keep us molten by virtue of our inner fire while our souls help us contain and direct our passion. Without spirit we congeal and die. Without soul we are unable to hold the tension of being molten and are pulled apart.

Soul helps us contain our basic passions in such a way that we can use their energy productively. More generally, we could say that soul helps us hold our experience. Our joys, our disappointment, our hopes, our fears, our excitement, our confusion, our suffering, and much more all need to be held in awareness. The alternative is to exclude troublesome experiences from consciousness through repression, but we have already seen how that leads to fragmentation, not integration. Holding these negative experiences in awareness provides the soul with its most fertile soil for growth as these things offer us an invitation to embrace life as it actually comes to us. The call of soul is always a call back to this place of being anchored in the realities of life and allowing the meaning of our own life to emerge from this place. No personal meaning that is found anywhere else will be of much use in the real world.

We usually have less trouble holding positive experiences than negative ones, but even these can at times be overwhelming. Holding joy, excitement, or anticipation expands the soul. Think, for example, about the typical four-year-old's ability to contain the excitement of Christmas Eve and how this contrasts with that of the typical fourteen-year-old. For most children, those intervening years involve growth in the capacity to contain arousal. We can think of this growth as development of the soul, or better, development of our capacity for the soul-function of holding experience.

For most adults, containing excitement is much easier than containing anxiety, despair, fear, or emotional pain. Even tension can be hard to hold. To seek to eliminate all tension is to seek escape from life. Our desires are always bigger than any possible satisfactions, and so there will always be within us a dis-ease that results in tension. The soul's task is to contain this tension. Jacques Lacan, the brilliant French psychoanalyst, suggests that it is soul that enables us to bear what is intolerable in the world.[3] There will always be plenty of this to be contained. Soul is what makes it possible to face the obvious lack of fairness in the world. Soul allows us to hold the evil, pain, and suffering that we see all around us and not be overwhelmed. Despair or acting out are the alternatives to containment. But our souls grow as we practice holding the tension associated with the lack of fairness and justice in a world that doesn't run as reason or social ideals suggest it ought.

Another source of tension is, of course, the fire in our belly. Personal experience demonstrates that containing our passions can be quite challenging. Our sexuality is, of course, part of this. Although Freud was wrong in thinking that our life instinct was reducible to sexuality, he was right in identifying sexuality as central to it. The soul's job is to hold the tension associated with our sexuality and passions as it seeks to contain, support, and channel our vital energies.

James Hillman describes soul as the middle ground between matter and spirit.[4] It exists in the space between events and experience, mind and body. It is neither physical and material nor spiritual and abstract. Yet it is bound to both. Soul resides in the reflective space between us and the events of our lives, between the doer and the deed. It is a way of seeing with depth. Soul makes meaning possible by connecting spirit to experience. Closely connected to death, it is inherently open to potential help that religion and spirituality offer for living life in the face of death. Standing in this middle ground, then, it plays a vital role in holding us together and in grounding us in life in the world, in the body, in the thick of things—including the dark, painful, messy, and confusing parts of life. The soul's connection to the dark and painful places explains, of course, why at times we want to escape it. At the same time, however, it also makes clear why a spiritual flight from this place can only lead to the disaster of a life that is no longer tethered to material realities.

The Journeys of Spirit and Soul

While the soul makes its home in the deep, shaded valley, spirit seeks a place in the bright light on the mountaintop. Describing the place of soul, the Dalai Lama says that "heavy torpid flowers saturated with black grow there. The rivers flow like warm syrup." In contrast, the dwelling place of spirit is "a land of high, white peaks and glittering jewel-like lakes and flowers."[5] The soul is at home in the mundane details of daily existence while the spirit pursues cosmic heights. The call of spirit is up and out, beyond our self, to places of self-transcendence and spaciousness. Soul, on the other hand, calls us down and in to a place of groundedness within the realities of our lives and the human condition.

The upward and outward thrust of spirit is a journey of longing and of movement toward self-transcendent soaring. Spirit is expansive, always questing, driven by deep longings. In religious spiritualities the ultimate reference point for this longing is often understood as Other— something so totally beyond the self that it is sometimes called the Wholly Other. Ultimately, I believe we seek relationship between self and the self-transcendent, this being, of course, the source of religion. The place of encounter with that which is beyond our individual self is a place that allows us perspective on life. Here we transcend the particulars of our own small, often cramped, lives. In relationship to the transcendent, we find our personal meaning. We find our place. And, as we shall see, this place will always be a place that invites surrender.

In contrast, the call of soul is a call to belonging, descent, and grounding. Soul penetrates the particularities of our life. It invites us to learn what the lessons of triumph and achievement can never teach us. Only suffering and struggle, and all the dark experiences that come with them, will grow a soul big enough to hold our life. This happens when we ground ourselves in the blood, sweat, and tears of ordinary life. Rather than rising above these things, soul calls us to find life and meaning in the midst of them.

However, describing the journeys of spirit and soul separately obscures the fact that they intersect in important ways. The journey of soul constantly invites engagement with the journey of spirit, and vice versa. Spiritual journeys that are not grounded in these fundamental dimensions of soulful living will always be superficial, and a spiritual quest that seems blocked is often a quest that needs to pay more attention to these challenges of soulful living. Similarly, journeys of soulful living that do not connect a person to a self-transcendent reference point ultimately provide an inadequate framework for integration of personhood. Thomas Moore notes that "without the deep soul the spirit risks cutting itself off from humanity. Swept away by the spirit, we'd like to become angels, but steeped in the soul we'd like a good meal with friends. The soul tames ambition, which can be one of the great dangers of the spirit. Without depth, spirit can be dangerously volatile, like spirits in chemistry that can blow up. Without the ballast of the soul, the spirit drafts, floats and zooms away from the earth."[6]

The journeys of spirit and soul should complement each other. Under ideal circumstances, we will be unable to tell the difference between them. However, such ideal circumstances pass quickly, and we are once again aware of what seems like a call to two separate but closely interrelated journeys. Both, however, make an indispensable contribution to the process of becoming fully human.

Soulful Living

Since the idea of living with soul may be unfamiliar—and the language somewhat strange—perhaps a helpful starting point would be two concepts that will likely be more familiar: soul food and soul music.

Most ethnic groups have what they call soul food. In the United States, the term is usually associated with African Americans and the food that is connected to their roots as slaves in America. As slaves, they had to make do with whatever food was available, this often being nothing more than what had been discarded from the plantation house. After the abolition of slavery, this food continued to be the way of staying in contact with their heritage.

Soul food uses everything available and combines it in ways that have been associated with one's cultural heritage. Nothing is wasted. Nothing is fancy. Soul food is simple food prepared in an uncomplicated manner—food that is good for body and soul. Likewise, soul music contains many of the same ingredients. And once again, it turns up in most cultures. Usually melancholic and nostalgic, soul music takes the form of songs of love, longing, and loss. It is music of the people. And it is grounded in the existential realities of life.

Some people who feel no connection whatsoever to the notion of spirituality feel an intuitive understanding of the idea of food that nourishes the soul or music that is its language. They might also speak with passion about the soul of the nation, the soul of their people, or even the soul of the earth. They seem to recognize that certain things are good for the soul and others are not—even if they do not always follow this inner compass. And they seem to be aware of the soul's call and strive to be responsive to it. They seek to live with authenticity, love, and awareness while remaining anchored in the realities of their life. This is soulful living.

Soul thrives in reality but quickly withers when we live in places of illusion or denial. Soul, as we have seen, provides a container in which we can hold reality—both pleasant and unpleasant aspects of it. It hosts our reception of the pleasant and desirable aspects of experience and allows joy and gratitude to develop as a response. But it also holds the parts of our experience that we would never choose—things such as suffering, loss, and despair. These form the most fertile soil for the growth of soul as they offer us an invitation to face and even embrace life as it actually comes to us, not as we would arrange it if we actually were the masters of our own destiny. The call of soul is always a call back to this place of being anchored in the realities of life as it actually is, so that we can allow the meaning of our own life to emerge from this place. No personal meaning that is found anywhere else will be of much use in the real world.

An authentic life is a simple life. This does not mean that it is easy or that the people who are authentic are simplistic, uninteresting, or unintelligent. Rather, it means that such people are integral. The various strands of their being all work together. What you see is what you get—no pretense, no games, just the simple truth of their being. This is the elegance of the authentic life and is a hallmark of soulful living.

Authenticity is one of the by-products of a commitment to a firm embrace of reality. Body and soul contain thousands of possibilities out of which you can build many identities. But only one of these will be your true self. This, Dag Hammarskjöld argues, you will never find "until you have excluded all those superficial and fleeting possibilities of being and doing with which you toy out of curiosity or wonder or greed, and which hinder you from casting anchor in the experience of the mystery of life, and the consciousness of the talent entrusted to you which is your I."[7] Your authentic self will always be unique. But it will never be a uniqueness you simply choose. It is the self you—in truth—already are. Living this truth is living soulfully.

Although they would seldom use this language, many people I work with in psychotherapy come for help in living soulfully. They want more than treatment of their emotional and psychological problems; they also want assistance in living the simple truth of their being.

Nick—a very successful venture capital manager in his late thirties—is a good example of this. He had made more money in the first decade of his working life than most of us will make in a lifetime. But, although he had been tempted by the seductions of an inflated lifestyle and sense of his own importance, he lived a remarkably grounded and authentic life. He lived on 10 percent of his income, giving the rest to his foundation for philanthropic work. He had no religious involvement, nor did he think of himself as spiritual. He did, however, want to live his life with integrity, so he approached me for help in making some decisions that he faced during the course of a messy divorce. His lawyers were working with him to keep as many of his assets intact as possible. What he wanted from me was help in ensuring that his soul remained intact. He put it in terms of not losing his way. His way—and his focus—had been what he described as the greatest good for the greatest number. He wanted his life to add value to the world. This was his spirituality.

I often stand in awe of the lives that people working with me have created out of the raw materials they were given. I am not easily impressed by wealth or power, but I am deeply impressed by people who find a way to live their life with integrity, authenticity, courage, honesty, and creative engagement with their needs and those of others and the world. When I look carefully I see patterns of personal meaning that are not just associated with present experience and life circumstances but with reference points that are transcendent to self. I hear longings that point beyond the self and lead to the transformation of an ordinary life into an extraordinary one.

Byram Karasu—one of the few authors to explore the relationship between soulful and spiritual living—suggests that soulfulness involves the transformation of the extraordinary to the ordinary by love, while spirituality involves the transformation of the ordinary to the extraordinary by belief.[8] Spirit and soul are both involved in alchemical processes of transformation. Both deal with the ordinary and the extraordinary. The ordinary is ultimately best engaged when we allow it to be a doorway to the experience of the extraordinary. And the extraordinary only serves us well when it leads us back into the midst of the ordinary. Meaning, it appears, must be found and lived in both places.

Just as soul food and soul music are grounded in particular cultures, so too is soulful living grounded in one's unique heritage and culture. We are not defined by either heritage or culture, but both form part of our reality—the ground out of which we emerge and grow. If we lose contact with this ground, we are doomed to a life of pretense. Soulful living calls us to remember who we are and where we have come from. This is the essential foundation for a life of authenticity.

Soulful living is also living with awareness. There can be no real groundedness or authenticity apart from awareness. Awareness connects us to present realities within the self and the environment. It then predisposes us to action. Soulful living does not just make us aware of inner and outer realities but engages us with them in ways that enhance life for ourselves and others. This means we learn to relate to our self and the world with love—for without love, life can never be genuinely full and fulfilling.

Longing and Belonging

Soulful living involves not only connection and meaning but also belonging. But belonging never stands alone. Its partner, longing, is always nearby. Life is lived on the dance floor in the space between longing and belonging. Soulful spirituality does not move you onto the dance floor. It merely makes you mindful of where you are.

The longing to belong is at the heart of our nature. In his book *Eternal Echoes*, John O'Donohue suggests that "the word 'belonging' holds together the two fundamental aspects of life: Being and Longing, the longing of our Being and the being of our Longing."[9] Longing points us toward a mooring beyond the self that prevents us from falling into ourselves. That place is a place of belonging.

There is a constant and vital tension between longing and belonging. O'Donohue describes this tension with eloquence: "Without the shelter of belonging, our longings would lack direction, focus and context; they would be aimless and haunted, constantly tugging the heart in a myriad of opposing directions. Without belonging, our longing would be demented. As memory gathers and anchors time, so does belonging shelter longing. Belonging without longing would be empty and dead, a cold frame around emptiness."[10]

Longing can atrophy under conditions of overly comfortable belonging—particularly a nostalgic belonging that is grounded more in the past than in the emerging present. But longings can be so strong and a sense of belonging so weak that one is left rootless. I sometimes think of this in relation to a kite. For proper flight, a kite needs a string that grounds it. Without the tension produced by this grounding it may continue to be blown by the wind, but it won't soar with the energy that comes when one end is firmly anchored to the ground. But a kite is not, of course, merely a string. Without the broad, open expanse within which it catches the wind, it would also never fly. Soaring comes from longings that are matched by belongings—when we fly on the wind of spirit yet remain anchored in body and soul.

Soulful Spirituality

To describe a person's spirituality as soulful is not to identify it with one particular spiritual path. Soulful spirituality is not a path but a way of walking the human path. It is a way of living that orients the individual toward life as it is encountered in their body and in the flow of their lived experience. It is a way of living that is essential if we are to become fully human. It is a way of living out of the depths of our being that orients us to the potential heights of our becoming.

Christian spirituality can be either soulless or soulful. The same is true of Buddhist, New Age, 12-step, or any other spirituality—religious or nonreligious. Soulful spirituality is living out our spiritual journey in a way that helps us become deeply and authentically human. In contrast, soulless spirituality is any spirituality that diminishes our capacity for actualization of the potentials of human personhood.

It may sound a bit soulless of me to use such strong language to describe spiritual paths that lead us away from humanness. But in doing so I am employing the common understandings of the word. To be soulless, in popular language, is to be insensitive or inhuman. Think of what might be called soulless organizations. Generally, this would refer to organizations that are not sensitive to human needs and human realities—or more specifically, not good for humans! That is exactly the point I wish to make. Soulless spirituality is not good for humans. In contrast, soulful spirituality is spirituality that nourishes human life and fosters human development.

Soulful spirituality channels our vitality in a way that integrates and orients us toward the transcendent. It guides our response to our deepest longings and provides the framework within which our life becomes meaningful. It can never be reduced to practices, but it shapes our lives and in that sense must be lived, not simply believed. In subsequent chapters we will be discussing it in much more detail—particularly in part 3, where we will examine specific practices of soulful spirituality.

Living Soulfully and Spiritually

Take a few minutes to reflect on the issues addressed in this chapter. The capacity for reflection on experience is one of the hallmarks of a healthy soul, and the exercise of this capacity is itself an important psychospiritual practice.

> ⚜ Think about the way in which you manage the fire in your belly and respond to your deepest longings to find your place in relation to the self-transcendent. But think also about your attentiveness to the cultivation of the womb of your experience and your response to the call to live a life that is grounded in the mundane details of ordinary experience. Soulful spirituality balances the ordinary and the extraordinary—each leading to a fuller engagement with the other. In general, which dimension of your inner life—the journey of spirit or the journey of soul—is most in need of your attention at present?

- ✤ How do your longings and belongings balance each other? Being careful not to blame external circumstances, what keeps your life from soaring? What keeps your spirituality grounded?
- ✤ Finally, which aspects of soulful living that you encountered in this chapter feel most deficient in your life? Which came with the strongest sense of invitation? How do you wish to respond to any such invitations?

The human journey is, in reality, singular—not divisible into separate journeys of spirit and soul. Yet paying attention to both dimensions is important as we easily neglect one or the other at the expense of our whole being. As we will see in the next chapter, spirit and soul are intertwined in the human journey, every step of psychological development pregnant with spiritual significance and none of them possible apart from spiritual response.

5

The Spiritual Nature of the Human Journey

The human journey to full personhood takes a lifetime and can never be fully completed until death. Death is not simply the end of life but the last stage of life. It is an important part of the journey.

Spirituality is essential to this journey—to the whole of it. Erik Erikson's map of human development clearly illustrates this. For each of eight stages he identified a developmental crisis that must be faced and a spiritual way of living that results from the successful resolution of this crisis. Hope, for example, is the outcome associated with the successful resolution of the first crisis of infancy.[1] This crisis is built around the choice between trust and mistrust. But hope is not simply a virtue, like telling the truth. It is an orientation to life. It emerges out of the child's primal perception of the quality of the attachment to caretakers. If this attachment is sufficiently secure it will lead to a sense of safety that, in turn, will become the psychological core of the spiritual posture of hope. Similarly, courage, purpose, self-worth, fidelity, love, and the commitment to make a social contribution and live a life of wisdom are all spiritual postures associated with successive stages of psychological development.

Stages of the Journey

For purposes of our overview of development there is no need for such a detailed map of life stages. There has been a long tradition across many cultures of dividing the journey to personhood into two broad stages, and these should serve us well. In the first stage, lasting from childhood to midlife, our focus is primarily external. This is when we learn the ways of the world and make our way in relation to the demands of family, work, and society. In the second stage, we turn more inward and begin to create a system of personal meaning that is based not so much on what we can do but on who we are. The primary task of the first stage of life is the development of ego, and the challenge of the second stage is relativizing and transcending it. The first involves ego separation from what Jung called the *Self*, while the second involves movement back toward union with Self. The Self—a concept I will explain shortly—anchors the human journey and, as we shall see, makes it thoroughly spiritual.

While both religion and psychology have a clear interest in this journey, and both make important contributions to our understanding of it, psychology has focused more on the first stage and task (developing ego), whereas religion has focused more on the second (relativizing and transcending ego). In both, however, spirituality plays a central role. In this chapter, we will explore the broad contours of this journey, focusing on the development of the ego and the subsequent challenge of bringing it into alignment with the Self.

Saint Paul gives us an overview of what that realignment looks like when he says, "I have been crucified with Christ, and I live now not with my own life but with the life of Christ who lives in me" (Gal. 2:20). In this statement Paul says that his personality has been radically reorganized—a reorganization that was sufficiently drastic for him to speak of it in terms of death and new life. His new life, he says, no longer revolves around his ego but around a larger center within himself that he describes as "Christ who lives in me." This is the reorganization of the inner life that we will examine, a reorganization in which the ego moves from the star role to that of a supporting actor.

But even ego is not present at birth. It develops out of a more primitive self. It is with this original self that we begin our story.

The Original Self

Following Jung and others, we might call the self that exists at birth *Self*. The capitalization of this word denotes the fact that this is something vastly bigger than what we experience or think of as "me." The Self is both the center and the circumference of our being. It is the totality of our personality, including both the conscious and the unconscious. It is more than we can consciously experience because it is so much more than our individuality. Here we are one with our Origin, for this is the dimension of our being that is already in harmony with God, already in God. Here we are most deeply our true self, the self I have described as our self-in-God.[2]

To use more theological language, we could say that the Self is the *imago Dei*—the imprint of the Divine that we are. It is here that we are at one with God, where the human and the Divine meet in the depths of the psyche. Here we are also at one with all that is. This is the sacred space into which we are first born. At this point there is no ego. In the beginning all is Self.

Because this original Self is at one with all that is, our earliest experience of self and the world is not an experience of "I" versus "it" or "them," but of "we."[3] It is an experience of wholeness. Observing mother and infant, it is often easy to see something of the mutuality, union, and bliss that this involves. Often there appears to be no psychic dividing line between the two parties. The young child may take food out of his mouth and put it into his mother's. The mother will often do the same, not feeling disgust but instead experiencing a thrilling sense of unity. Provided she is sufficiently mature in her own psychological development, she knows, of course, that the sense of union masks the reality that they are two individuals, not one. However, at this point the infant is incapable of knowing this.

During the first few months, mother and newborn must begin to replace the physical oneness of the womb with psychological oneness. Bridging the gap between biological and psychological oneness requires the cooperation of the mother and father (or caretakers) and the newborn. The mother's role in reaching out to the newborn and allowing each to attach to the other is of central importance.[4] Thankfully, most mothers find this task relatively easy. All that is needed is her presence and her ability to respond to the infant's helplessness. The infant's mottled skin, unfocused eyes, cute fat cheeks, occasional smile, and uncoordinated movements cry out for a mother to touch and hold her newborn. In that holding, body and spirit of mother and infant become attuned to each other, and the infant begins to develop the soul capacity to hold his or her own experience.

The holding that the mother provides is not simply physical but is more fundamentally a state of attunement to the infant's needs. "Holding" is everything that mothers do for their infant that produces a sense of wholeness and well-being. It includes both the coming together of their bodies and the times when they are apart. Over time, both can feel and remain deeply connected even when physically separated. This is one of the most important differences between psychological and biological oneness.

Most newborns achieve a state of psychological oneness with their mother by the end of the first month of their life. Soon a sense of a unique self will emerge out of this undifferentiated state of union. But while this state of feeling at one with all that is does not last long, it is extremely powerful. It shapes all subsequent longing. Wisps of memory of this archetypal belonging will be part of every subsequent act of identification of self with something larger than self—a political party, social movement, religious tradition, sports team, or country. Each of these belongings will be motivated by the unconscious memory of the way in which our original self was at one with everything beyond it—a memory that reminds the autonomous ego of its alienation from this original state of at-oneness.

The earliest experiences of infants with their mothers are also where we learn, or fail to learn, about the basic trustworthiness of others and the safety of the world. Given a good enough base of trustworthy love and nurture, we move toward the sense that despite inevitable frustrations and hurts, the world is not implacably hostile to us. If this initial attachment is not secure, all subsequent attachments will be fraught with danger. But if this initial attachment helps us trust that we can exist with safety within a larger relational nexus, our life force will be strengthened as we leave the womb of undifferentiated union. That will prepare us for midlife when we will have an opportunity to journey back to the place where our sense of identity is anchored in this larger Self.

From We to Me

The infant's experience of union with mother in the first several months is so complete that there is scarcely an awareness of separate identities. Everything that the infant perceives at this stage is perceived as being within the self. The bliss, harmony, and pleasure—or displeasure—that come from being fed and held are experienced as if they are internally produced. This delusion of being at one with everything in the outer world is tremendously empowering. It provides the battered self that emerges from the rupturing of biological oneness with a sense of power and well-being. Perhaps, after all—the infant may conclude—there may be life after the rupture. And it might even be as blissful as that which preceded it.

Inevitably, however, awareness of separateness begins to develop. This dawning realization of the separateness of mother and the external world forms an important transition step in the infant's movement from an inner focus to an external one. This awareness need not be traumatic. The two individuals can remain in a harmonious unity that recognizes separateness but holds them together in spite of this. This first awareness of separateness is the point where ego enters the picture.

At first, ego is simply the sense of the me that is separate from mother or the primary caretaker. The establishment of this boundary between me and not-me is foundational to all subsequent psychological and spiritual development. Confusion or uncertainty about what is me and what is not-me means that the person will live life in a psychotic fog.

The differentiation of ego from non-ego is initially quite crude. The earliest iterations of me are little more than a collection of part-selves based on fragments of experience. Similarly, other people who form the largest figures on the not-me horizon are perceived in only the most general terms. It will take quite some time before these inner fragments begin to coalesce and self and others are experienced as integrated wholes. In fact, some people never achieve this as a stable platform. They will spend the rest of their lives working toward the elusive goal of an integrated sense of self and others.

Ego and Self

While earliest awareness of the boundaries of ego usually begins to appear several months after birth, this awareness is not complete until sometime around eighteen months of age—a point often called our *psychological birth*.[5] This is the moment when the infant's sense of being a separate identity—of having an "I" or being "me"—is usually in place. It is a crucially important developmental accomplishment because without ego there can be no self. However, while this is progress in terms of movement toward a mature self, it also involves a loss. Ego is partial and frail, but it believes itself to be whole and absolute. Cut off from Self, it leaves us in a place of isolated individuality—a fragment of a branch broken from the tree that is our true life.

Soon this loss gets even greater. Ego is the part of my experience with which I consciously identify. It becomes, therefore, the center of the conscious mind around which I organize everything else. As this happens, however, I lose contact with the wholeness that includes both the conscious and the unconscious elements. My sense of self becomes, therefore, even smaller. I increasingly identify with the contents of consciousness—primarily thoughts and emotions. In a short period of time I have moved from a sense of "me" that is totally identified with the larger Self to a sense of "me" that is now totally identified with what I experience as my thoughts, my emotions, my memories, and my body.

Ego is a usurper. It takes the place of Self as our center, but it cannot fill its shoes. It is an illusory self. It pretends to be the true self but is nothing more than a facade that masks the small and often rather empty place behind it. Ego does have some very important roles to play in personality, and we will examine these later. However, because it is rooted in our individuality, it lacks the fundamental sense of solidarity with others and with the world that is part of life in the Self. We may pretend to care for that which is beyond us, and may even feel that we truly do, but such feelings will be superficial. They no longer spring from our depths but arise instead from the small place that we now make our home—ego.

This task of reconnecting with our larger and truer self is the task of spirituality. Better, we could say that the gift of spirituality is the connection between ego and Self. This connection allows us to soften the boundaries of ego and get beyond the isolation of the small place that it represents. It is the journey of freeing ourselves from the illusion that we are merely separate egos set apart from each other and from God, discovering instead that, once released from the prison of individuality we are one with God, one with all that is. The gift of the spiritual journey is the recovery of our deep longing to belong and to surrender in relationship to someone or something transcendent, a longing that is very dim and distant when we are imprisoned in our egos.

John Sanford, an Episcopal priest and Jungian analyst, offers a helpful analogy for thinking about the relationship of ego and Self. He suggests that we can compare the ego to the neck of a bottle of wine and the Self to the wine that fills the bottle. Clearly, it is the wine that is important, the only value of the neck of the bottle being that it allows the wine to get out. "The ego is like this," he says. "It is either like the neck of the bottle through which the wine of the Self flows, or it becomes an obstruction to the process in which case we might speak of its being a bottleneck, an impediment."[6] But, more precisely, it is not the ego that causes the bottleneck. Despite how it is often presented, ego is not the great enemy of the spiritual life. That enemy is egocentricity.

Egocentricity

Generations of hatred between Protestants and Roman Catholics in Ireland have produced the Irish aphorism that hatred comes from mother's milk. Something akin to this inevitable passage of hatred from generation to generation appears to happen with egocentricity. Regardless of how much love any of us received as children, it is never the right kind of love. Inevitably, to one degree or another, it is always egocentric, conditional, and incomplete. No parent can avoid passing on love that is colored by their own ego needs and limitations. Our egocentricity is the inevitable response to drinking this egocentric milk from an early age.

Without ever having experienced perfect love, all of us seem to have an archetypal sense of what it is and what it would be like—and no love that we experience can ever measure up to the standard this represents. Each generation passes this inadequate love on to the next. And in so doing, each generation predisposes the next to become even more egocentric.

Egocentricity is a defense against the inadequacies of the love we all receive. It is a response to the narcissistic injuries that we inevitably experience while growing up. These injuries are anything that threaten our sense of well-being or diminish our feelings of self-worth. For the infant, this might be a delayed feeding or change of a wet diaper. For the young child, it might be a taunt from a playmate or an unfair criticism from a parent or teacher. It does not take most children long to learn to defend against these assaults on their fragile self.

Egocentricity is the first line of that defense. It is our way of trying to protect our ego from further damage, something that we sense to be absolutely essential because ego feels like the very core of our being. This is, of course, an illusion. Ego is an important part of us, but it is far from our totality or essence. It is, in fact, a dreadfully inadequate substitute for our true center—the Self.

But notice that it is not ego that is damaged by these assaults to Self. It is self-esteem. Egocentricity is the bandage we wrap around our self-esteem when it feels wounded and fragile. Far from being a mark of an ego that is too strong, egocentricity is a mark of a fragile and vulnerable ego.

This metaphor of a bandage also helps us see how egocentricity cuts us off from the source of our life when the bandage is too tight. That source of life is the Self—our larger and truer Self as it exists in relationship to the transcendent. The development of ego represents a move in the direction of alienation from our deep center in the Self. This is why the ego is less vital and more superficial than the Self. But when the bandage of egocentricity is tightly wrapped around our wounded self we are even further deprived of the life-giving supply of nutrients that comes from the Self. Cut off from the Self, we begin to suffer a lack of vitality, creativity, compassion, and sense of solidarity with all humans.

Egocentricity is the ego turning back in upon itself, rather than opening in trust to others and the world. It is a revolt against the openness, mutuality, and fellowship of life in the Self. As soon as egocentricity enters the picture, the ability of the young child to experience others as a part of the Self is diminished. If it gains enough traction in the child's life, it may well snuff out entirely this capacity for empathy and love. We can, of course, continue to be in relationships with others, but until egocentricity is resolved we will not experience the deep connectedness that is possible when ego is grounded in Self.

Paradoxically, egocentricity is also turning away from our own depths—from all that does not fit with the false self we are creating in the image of who we think we want to be or, at least, want to be seen as. This means it involves an alienation from our unconscious. But that which we choose to ignore is that which will subsequently tyrannize us. Our freedom never comes from ignoring that which does not comfortably fit with the self we would like to be. It comes from an embrace of the total truth of who we, in reality, are.

Life gets seriously out of balance under the influence of egocentricity. Penultimate goods that should be only a means to an end in the service of Self become ultimate goods that are detached from their proper relationship to life. Thus, for example, money, power, esteem, or success may be accepted by an egocentric person as being of ultimate value. But when penultimate things are elevated to places of ultimacy, the soul is always damaged.

Egocentricity is singularly capable of destroying our life. It alienates us from our own true self and from others. It leaves us imprisoned in a small place, starving for the vitality that can only come from our Source. It propels us toward spiritual crisis.

The Crisis

Egocentricity ultimately destroys the life that it appears to protect. Forced to do a job it was never intended or equipped to do, our ego becomes increasingly brittle and hollow. Deprived of the life-giving nutrients that flow from a relationship with our Source and cut off from the vitality of our deeper Self, it is simply too small for the demands it faces. Consequently, egocentricity ultimately leads to a crisis.

For most people, this crisis is experienced sometime during the years of midlife. This is often when we first encounter significant personal suffering as adults—such things as losses, injustices, financial setbacks, interpersonal failures, or betrayals. These and other similar things challenge the adequacy of our system of personal meaning. By this point in life most of us have also often lost solid contact with our depths and with the transcendent heights that exist beyond us. The focus on success in the external world that so easily preoccupies us in the first half of life blinds us to our growing internal emptiness and to the increasing gap between inner realities and outer appearances.

James Hollis states that one of the most powerful shocks of what he calls the *middle passage* is the collapse of our implicit contract with the universe, "the assumption that if we act correctly, if we are of good heart and good intentions, things will work out."[7] We assume reciprocity with the universe, that if we do our part, the universe will comply. The midlife crisis is not so much the collapse of our selves as the collapse of these assumptions. It is a collapse of the way we have related to life—of our spirituality. It is a clash between the ego and the Self—that mysterious larger self that summons each of us to connect to the deep ground of our self and thereby become our true self. This is not the time to have an affair or change jobs or lifestyles in an attempt to save a drowning ego. It is a time to turn inward and establish contact with that which is beyond.

You may manage to make it through the middle years without experiencing anything like a crisis. You might, therefore, be tempted to scoff at the notion of the challenges of the middle passage of the journey. But don't be too quick to do so. The bill run up by a false self based on an egocentric life must be paid at some time, and if it doesn't come due in the middle years, it will come later. It may be triggered by the more major medical crises that we typically encounter in our seventh and eighth decades of life. Or it may simply be the insidious but inevitable erosion of vitality and well-being associated with aging that blows apart an inadequate sense of personal meaning.

Nietzsche once commented on how distressing it is to discover that you are not God. Eventually your egocentricity will result in your being knocked off balance because you are not the god that ego pretends to be. Eventually life will demand adjustments and new forms of adaptation that you will find impossible from the egocentric place you are living. How you respond to this will determine whether the crisis will ultimately be seen as a gift or as a curse.

The greater the degree of egocentricity, the more cracks will develop in the rigid ego that forms underneath the protective bandages. These cracks are the source of the crisis. They may be problems in our personal meaning, our engagement with reality, or even the adequacy of our management of our emotions or passions. Our capacity for creativity in avoiding these fractures is great, but the weight of life on the brittle shell of the ego will inevitably lead to some form of inner crisis. The longer we avoid dealing with the call to realign our lives that the crisis represents, the more serious it will eventually be.

Spiritual crisis is the only hope for the resolution of our egocentricity. It is the only route to the deep realignment of our self that is needed. The egocentric life has been built on an inadequate foundation, and there is no way to simply patch the cracks in that foundation. Egocentricity appears to be saving our life but is in fact destroying it. It is the major impediment to deep connections and vital living. It is the core of our spiritual and psychological dysfunction. It must die if we are to truly live. The only route to well-being is through the center of the crisis. There are no shortcuts.

Our natural reaction to any crisis, however, is to try and restore equilibrium—to do whatever possible to get ourselves back to where we were before things seemed to fall apart. But this won't work. That is why the crisis usually has to go through several ever-deepening cycles until we see that we have no alternative but fundamental change. Initially we think that our problems are caused by factors outside our selves. We may feel unfairly treated, and perhaps we were. Or we may feel that the crisis is simply the result of bad luck. But until we begin to see that the way we have organized our life—our spirituality—is the cause of our own distress, we are not ready to truly move through the crisis. To be ready to do so we must see that our very attempts to preserve our egocentric life are the cause of our problems. This is what Jesus taught when he said that if we genuinely desire to save our life we must first be prepared to lose it (Mark 8:34–36). This is the heart of the Paschal mystery—life emerges out of death. In order to save my life—that is, to really live—I must lose that which appears to be my life, the system of mistaken ideas and values that embody my ego.

Transformation

The pathway to the transformation of not only our egocentricity but our very self is the path of surrender. We must be willing to lay down that which we were previously willing to die to defend. But this surrender of egocentricity is not the same as the elimination of the ego. This is much confused in spiritual writings. Surrender of ego would be surrender of personhood, which is never appropriate. We cannot be human without ego, and we can never be fully human without a strong ego. In many people, ego is too weak for them to engage in meaningful surrender. This is the reason that psychotherapy must often first focus on ego strengthening. Without a strong and healthy ego we cannot engage in the transformational journey of ego relativization through surrender of egocentricity and the reestablishment of a life-giving connection to Self.

Ego has many important roles to play even when it is aligned with the larger Self. The ego includes all those mental functions that allow us to perceive, organize, elaborate, differentiate, integrate, and transform experience. Ego is a fundamental psychic structure that secures our reality testing, good judgment, impulse control, defensive functions, affective regulation, interpersonal relations, moral orientation, thought processes, and much more. It is essential to life, even the spiritual life. But it cannot fulfill the role that it is uniquely equipped to fill while it functions as chief executive officer. The Self—that is, our larger self that finds its place in relationship to the transcendent—must be the CEO. Then ego can become an outstanding COO, chief operating officer, working under but in close relationship with the Self.

The realignment of life that the crisis of egocentricity invites is ultimately a deeply spiritual matter. It involves dethroning the ego and replacing it in the executive role with something more transcendent and genuinely ultimate. In so doing we suddenly find our true self and we find our place in the larger whole. We discover that our life is not our own, but something that flows from a source infinitely greater than us. Suddenly we are connected with the foundations of not only our own life but human life in general—with the higher reality in whom we, and all humans, live and move and have our being. This happens, in Jung's words, "when the ego-will submits to God's will."[8] The result is the new life described by Saint Paul as the life of Christ who lives in us (Gal. 2:20). The ego is now governed by the Spirit displayed in Jesus when, just before his death, he said to his Father, "Let it be as you, not I, would have it" (Mark 14:36). This is a posture of life, not an accomplishment. It is a process, not an end point. It is a spiritual way of living in which the ego is consciously directed by the true and deep ground of our being.

Reflecting on the Journey

While the things we have discussed in this chapter have been of a more theoretical nature, they do have important personal implications. Take a few moments to reflect on the following questions as a way of processing some of these:

- I have argued in this chapter that egocentricity cuts us off from our truest self and the source of our life. What do you know about your own egocentricity and the ways in which it cuts you off from the larger wholeness in which you exist?
- What experiences have you had that have confronted you with the fact that you are not the god that ego pretends to be? How have you responded to them?
- How well aligned are your ego and your larger Self? How do you react to the suggestion that ego must ultimately be dethroned if it is to do its proper job and you are to reestablish a life-giving connection to your larger Self?

Every step in the human developmental journey is spiritual because humans are fundamentally constituted to live in relationship to a self-transcendent horizon. We may not always be aware of that horizon, but something in us reminds us that we are neither our own source nor our own fulfilment. How we respond to that larger-than-self horizon defines our spirituality and directs our developmental journey of becoming fully human.

6

Deep Religion and
Healthy Spirituality

Two important issues have been lurking on the sidelines of our discussion, and it is time to bring them onto center stage. First, God has crept into our conversation on a number of occasions; consequently, it is important that we examine the relationship between religion and spirituality. Second, the notion of healthy versus unhealthy spirituality has been raised at several points; we need, therefore, to look more closely at the criteria for distinguishing between the two. Now is a good time to do both as we turn in this chapter and the next to an examination of how we express our spirituality.

Religion and Spirituality

Religion and spirituality are intrinsically connected. Although they can be separated from each other, this always involves significant loss. In the most general terms, religion is the communal and creedal expression of spirituality that orients individuals to the sacred and the Divine. Much more than being simply one expression of spirituality, religion has for millennia been *the* container for spirituality. Religion without spirituality is an empty shell. It has lost its meaning, its spirit, and its life. This is the conclusion of many formerly religious people who now define themselves as spiritual but not religious. They see no hope in restoring spirituality to institutional religion, which seems to them not even to have noticed that spirituality has taken its leave.

However, because spirituality is broader than religion, it needs the container that religion provides. Otherwise, the journey toward the transcendent has no shape and no direction. While it is obvious that people can pursue the call of spirit apart from religion, no one can proceed very far on the spiritual journey without a commitment to a specific spiritual tradition. To fail to do so is to remain something of a spiritual dilettante—exploring a variety of expressions of spirituality but failing to face the hard lessons that come with commitment to one path and to the other people sharing that path.

This is the journey of many of the formerly religious who describe themselves as spiritual. One friend who places himself in this category says that the only significant thing he lost when he left the church to follow a self-designed spiritual path was community. He meditates, reads spiritual books from a number of traditions, uses his journal as a reflective space for his journey, and is always glad to talk with people about spirituality—but he lacks the sense of walking the path with others. This is a significant loss that has left him somewhat unanchored as he drifts from one spiritual practice to another, from one spiritual tradition to another.

Religion holds unique potential as a force of healing and integration, but it can also be in the service of repression and dissociation. It can provide the means of transforming the ordinary into the extraordinary, but it can also become a way to escape the drudgery of the ordinary at the expense of a strong embrace of reality. It can teach us how to journey through the great mysteries of life—such things as love, loss, sex, failure, and suffering—but it can also eliminate the mystery and transformational potency of any of these. In short, it can support either soulful or soulless spirituality.

Deep Religion

The English word *religion* is derived from the Latin *religare*, which means to "hold together" or "connect back." At its best, religion integrates and makes us more whole. It helps us hold together the tension of the disparate dimensions of our being—body, spirit, and soul; thought and emotion; being, doing, and becoming. It provides us with the broad contours of a story that has the potential to be big enough to make life meaningful, whatever comes our way. And it connects us back to the roots of our existence and of our shared humanity.

At its best, religion puts us in touch with the mystery of our being in relation to the transcendent. It provides a framework that allows us to be in contact with the power of the transcendent without blowing the circuits of the self. Religious spirituality involves a transformational process that touches all aspects of our being. It represents, therefore, an extremely valuable resource for healing our brokenness and making us more whole.

In the concluding chapter of *The Varieties of Religious Experience*, William James suggests that religion is a way of living that is expressed in terms of a trusting and open relationship with that which is beyond the self, zest that comes from a lyrical enchantment with the world, and an abiding sense of trust and peace.[1] I call this deep religion. It is the religious counterpart to soulful spirituality.

Deep religion orients us to the transcendent and helps us remain open to mystery. In contrast, shallow religion eliminates mystery and minimizes genuine transcendence. Deep religion teaches us to respond to the inscrutable with wonder and awe rather than with our default reaction of analysis and attempts at control. Deep religion grounds us in this life, never simply preparing us for whatever may come after death. It helps us live more honestly, fiercely, and courageously. It teaches us what it means to be human and how to live with authenticity, purpose, and meaning. By its rich use of symbols—the language of the unconscious—it engages us in our depths and helps us connect with the Divine in those deep places. In Thomas Moore's words, it puts us in touch with the "mythic and archetypal mysteries that shape our lives, and in that way we live from a profound place, as much engaged with the eternal as the temporal."[2] This is life with depth, breadth, and height.

Deep Religion and Soulful Spirituality

Those who pursue their spiritual journey within a religious context typically think of spirituality in much narrower terms than those who do not. Christians, for example, might understand their spirituality in terms of such practices as prayer, receiving the sacraments, or acts of social justice or charity and might assume that their spiritual journey started with the earliest rites of their religious life—conversion or baptism. In reality, however, everyone's spiritual journey begins long before these rites and is, at least potentially, much broader and deeper than can ever be experienced when one focuses only on religious practices. This broader place is soulful spirituality.

In part 3, I will devote one chapter to each of six practices of soulful spirituality—practicing awareness, cultivating wonder, honoring otherness, embracing reality, living with presence to the moment, and choosing surrender. These, as we shall see, are life practices that will ground a spiritual journey in the human journey and thereby help us become more whole and integral. However, with the possible exception of surrender, it would be easy to think of these foundations of spirituality as nonreligious. Some might not even think of them as spiritual. But viewed from the perspective of deep religion, they can be seen to be not just spiritual but profoundly religious.

Notice something important, though. None of these dimensions of soulful spirituality is the exclusive domain of any one religion. Rather, they are common to most religions. Some may be most immediately associated with one particular religion. For example, surrender is so integral to Christian spirituality that it might be assumed to be identical with it, just as awareness might be associated with Buddhist spirituality or honoring otherness with Judaism. However, as we shall see, each of these has an extremely important role to play in Christian spirituality and none is alien to any of the major religions.

These dimensions of spirituality are the underpinning of any life that strives to be both vital and meaningful. Without them, we are at risk of being adrift from the realities of our embodied existence and dangerously dissociated from the truth of our experience. With them, our awareness can include the self-transcendent, and our meaning, presence, and surrender can be organized around a relationship with the ground of our being.

I sometimes encounter Christians who feel stuck on their spiritual journey. Often they are frustrated by their lack of spiritual progress or discouraged by the shallowness of their experience of God. Instinctively they feel that what they must do is practice the Christian spiritual disciplines with more regularity and fervor. They are, therefore, usually surprised when I suggest that rather than pressing forward they step back and, at least for a while, focus on the foundational spiritual practices we have been considering. When religious spirituality lacks vitality and meaning, it is not usually because of a lack of spiritual discipline. More often than not it is because of a lack of attentiveness to the spiritual foundation.

Recently I led a six-day contemplative retreat for an ecumenical group of Christian clergy. Each day was built around one of the six dimensions of soulful spirituality. After a brief introduction to each dimension, I offered suggestions as to how participants could practice it for the rest of that day. The first day they spent becoming more aware. They were invited to do such things as find a leaf and engage it with all of their senses, or pay attention to their breathing, or practice an awareness scan of their bodies. The second day they built on this by practicing contemplative seeing of the world through eyes of wonder rather than reason. Each day they spent the majority of their waking hours in silence and solitude, practicing things that initially appeared to some of them to be nonreligious and of questionable applicability to their spiritual journey. Their response was, however, much like what I usually encounter. Let me quote from an email I received several months later from one of the participants who, for the first several days, was extremely suspicious of these seemingly silly practices.

> I can hardly believe the impact the retreat had on me. It changed my life, altering forever my experience of God and of the world. I am astounded that learning to truly see with my physical eyes can have such a profound impact on seeing with my spiritual ones. I could not imagine how a day spent attending to the otherness of those with whom I share my life changed how I encounter them now that I am back in my parish. It opened me to the traces of the Divine that lurk in the face of the other. I came thinking I needed a rest. I left knowing that what I really needed was to awaken. Thank you for helping me do so.

When the spiritual foundation is weak, any religious superstructure that might be built upon it will always be shaky. But when it is solid, any specifically religious practices that might be present will be more deeply meaningful.

Spirituality becomes explicitly religious when it begins to involve a personal relationship to a self-transcendent reference point for life. This point can be anything beyond the self that we invest with a sense of ultimacy—our Higher Power, our Supreme Good, our God. Our relationship with this transcendent reference point may be expressed in many ways, but in religious spirituality it will usually involve devotion or prayer. In other words, in religious spirituality we relate to the self-transcendent reference point in a personal manner.

Sometimes nonreligious spiritualities migrate toward a more religious expression. The more common direction of the drift seems, however, to be away from religious spirituality. Some people drift with apathy from the traditions of earlier life, while others leave with sadness as they conclude that churches, synagogues, mosques, and temples are no longer relevant to either their experience or their quest. Tragically, some leave not just dissatisfied but damaged.

Unfortunately, religious spirituality does not always live up to its promise. Religion has a huge shadow, and a failure to understand and integrate this often unacknowledged darkness leaves it vulnerable to the evil that lurks within it. It is important, therefore, neither to idealize religious expressions of the spiritual journey nor to lose sight of their unique potential.

However, it is not just religious spirituality that can be unhealthy. Nonreligious forms of spirituality can also fail to make us more fully human. For both religious and nonreligious forms, then, it is important to know how to distinguish between healthy and unhealthy expressions of spirituality. There are, I believe, at least three important criteria for doing so: the quality of our relationships, the nature of our faith and sense of belonging, and the sense of meaning that emerges from our relationship to the transcendent.

Loving Relationships

The spiritual life is a life of engagement and connection, not a life of isolation and alienation. But healthy spirituality involves a particular way of relating to others and to the world. It involves relating in love.

Healthy spirituality always grows out of and nurtures a love of life. If we do not truly love life, we will never fully love anything or anyone else. A genuine embrace of life makes it possible for us to embrace others. If, on the other hand, we are ambivalent about life, that ambivalence will permeate all other relationships.

The spiritual life starts with choosing life. Just before entering the promised land after wandering in the wilderness for a generation, God offered the children of Israel a stark choice: "I set before you life or death, blessing or curse. Choose life, then, so that you and your descendants may live, in the love of Yahweh your God" (Deut. 30:19–20). Choosing life is choosing love. And genuine love of life cannot remain for long as simply love of *my* life. Love of life is contagious. It spreads to all facets of my life, and it spreads to others. That is the nature of love. If I really love life, I cannot help but begin to value your life as well as mine. If I genuinely love life, I will treat all life as sacred. If I genuinely love life, I will care for the world because I care for the generations of humans who may yet be born.

Love is the summum bonum—the supreme good—in most major world religions. I believe it is particularly in Christian spirituality that we see love elevated to the highest place. Though this might be just what you would expect to hear from a Christian, it might perhaps be more surprising to hear the eminent Islamic scholar Khalifa Abdul Hakim make the same argument: "In Jesus we have the culminating point of that upward movement where God and religion are completely identified with love which has preference over all legalism and ritualism."[3] While he thinks that Christianity has strayed from what we encounter in the life and teaching of Jesus, he is clear in his call to Christians and Muslims alike to ground their spiritual life in this love that is exemplified in Jesus.

Jesus distilled the whole of the Jewish Decalogue (the Ten Commandments) into love. In response to a question from the Pharisees about which was the greatest commandment, Jesus answered, "You must love the Lord your God with all your heart, with all your soul, and with all your mind. This is the greatest and the first commandment. The second resembles it: You must love your neighbor as yourself. On these two commandments hang the whole Law, and the Prophets also" (Matt. 22:37–40). Love is God's supreme command—love of God, self, neighbor, and enemies (Matt. 5:43–44).

In Jesus's teaching, our relationships with others are inseparable from our love of God—two faces of the same coin. Love is to be the way others can recognize a Christ-follower (John 13:34–35). And just as love was the measure of his own life, so too Jesus made it the measure of human fulfillment and the supreme criterion of healthy spirituality.

Faith and Belonging

A sense of belonging is absolutely vital to human well-being. If your spirituality does not provide you with a deep awareness of belonging in life and in the world, it is not serving you well. But a feeling of belonging will always be grounded in an experience of safety and trust. Albert Einstein noted that the most important question any person will ever answer is whether the world is friendly. Everything else, he said, flowed from this.[4] It is only when the universe seems to be reasonably safe that we can relax in our engagement with life and experience belonging. Without this sense of basic trust, we will always be on guard against dangers and in tension with our longing to belong.

Faith begins with trust. Emotional trust is the foundation of spiritual faith. The one leads seamlessly into the other. Thomas Moore reminds us that "when parents and teachers have faith in children, young people pick up that faith like a contagion. They learn to deal with obstacles and face their lives with confidence. Giving this kind of faith to others is a key form of service and a major element in any spiritual life."[5]

The experience of belonging to those who love us is essential even to physical well-being. After reviewing several decades of burgeoning research on the relationship of spirituality and health, Dean Ornish summarized his findings by saying that no other factor in medicine— not diet, smoking, exercise, stress, genetics, or drugs—"has greater impact on our quality of life, incidence of illness, or possibility of premature death than love and intimacy."[6] Study after study has shown that people who feel isolated are much more likely to get sick and die prematurely when compared to those who have a sense of connection and community. Even the love of a pet can make all the difference in the world, as many who are isolated for health or others reasons have come to know. Belonging is essential for human well-being and is central to any healthy spirituality.

Faith is not merely for the religious. It is the trust that is present in the life of everyone who has a sense of belonging to someone or something. Belonging to something other than self is foundational to any healthy spirituality.

Transcendent Meaning

Humans are meaning-seeking creatures. We need to be able to tell ourselves a story that integrates new experiences within the narrative that we have constructed to make sense of old ones. We never achieve meaning in some final form. New experiences—particularly if they involve suffering or a reversal of fortunes—always demand that we revisit our meaning system and see how it can help us fit the new experience within our evolving life story.

I call it a life story rather than a worldview because it is not simply a story about the nature of the world in general. The meaning that we need if our lives are to have cohesion cannot be a set of theological or philosophical propositions. It cannot be a story about me as an abstraction, in isolation from the world. The story that I need for my life to be meaningful is a story that must connect me and my experience to everything that lies beyond me—the personal and the transpersonal, the immanent and the transcendent. It is this kind of a story that we need to make our moment-by-moment existence meaningful. Meaning must be both found and created, and both must happen within the context of our life as it unfolds.

A number of years ago I had a personal crisis that was largely of my own making but that, nonetheless, threw my life into a tailspin. Although there was a substantial emotional component to this (significant depression and a great deal of anxiety), what was spinning was largely my belief and meaning system. I had made serious errors in my judgment of others. I felt forced to reevaluate what I believed about myself and my capacity for good judgment, and about others and their trustworthiness. I felt betrayed, and the world felt less safe and hospitable. Moving through this experience gave me an opportunity for important updating of the framework that made my life meaningful. All life experiences do this, but some bring a greater sense of urgency to do it than others.

Our true spirituality is always the meaning we actually live, not the meaning to which we give cognitive or verbal assent. It is always expressed, therefore, in our behavior, not simply in our thoughts or inner commitments. What we say to others or ourselves will tell part of our story, but deeper parts of it will be reflected in how we actually live our life. Personal meaning is a lived story, not simply a believed story or a told story.

The absence of such lived meaning will appear in many places, but one of the first and most reliable is in boredom. How often you find yourself bored—or discover your restlessness leading to unfulfilling, compulsive behavior—tells the story about how useful a framework your meaning provides for your life. What you think constitutes your spiritual meaning may have little to do with what makes moment-by-moment living actually meaningful. This lived meaning is your actual, functional spirituality.

Ultimately, we need a meaning that will be strong enough to make suffering sufferable. This is the crucial test of any life-meaning. It has to help us live life. For it to do that, it has to help us cope with suffering, loss, and death.

If our spirituality is to make suffering bearable, it must first help us embrace the suffering, not fight it. Accepting suffering is a spiritual response because, except for the more unusual forms of suffering that we bring upon ourselves, suffering is beyond our control. Acceptance allows us to move beyond anger and resentment. It allows our meaning system to support us in the face of something beyond the limits of our power. It does this by inviting us to engage with the questions suffering asks of us. This is quite different from the questions we tend to ask when we suffer, which often boil down to two: why me? and why now? Unfortunately, these questions are unanswerable. The questions that suffering asks of us, in contrast, include things like the following:

- Why is this suffering such a surprise? Why did you ever expect to be free of pain?
- How else might you organize your life other than around the avoidance of pain and suffering?
- What might change if you were to accept your suffering rather than fight it? Why do you resist such acceptance?

Suffering gives us a chance to deepen our spiritual journey. For this to occur, we must befriend it, not simply endure it. This never happens automatically. On the contrary, everything within us resists befriending the pain and distress. However, if we do manage to succeed in getting rid of suffering before we have answered its questions, we miss the opportunity for growth that it represents.

Spirituality invites us to the development and deepening of a meaning of life, not merely a meaning of suffering. Any such meaning that has even a chance of being strong enough to help us face all that life brings is a meaning that will always have been fired in the hearth of suffering.

Taking Stock

Any genuinely soulful or healthy spirituality cannot simply be adopted from your family or acquired from your community or culture. It must arise as a personal response to your deepest longings and help you make sense of your actual life experiences. It will, therefore, always be dynamic—evolving and changing. To turn it into something rigid and fixed is always to render it soulless, for that which is no longer evolving is either devolving or dead.

Take some time to reflect on your own spirituality in light of the things discussed in this chapter. Be as honest as you can in this process. Notice what is, and don't confuse that with what you think it should be. Consider the following questions as a way to frame this reflection:

- ✢ In this chapter I suggested that deep religion provides us with a big enough story to make life meaningful, connects us to the roots of our existence and our shared humanity, brings us in touch with both the mysteries of our being and the transcendent source of our being, and provides us with a basis for a trusting and open relationship to the world and God. It also grounds us in our life in the world and helps us live with more honesty and courage. Furthermore, by its rich use of symbols, deep religion engages us in our depths and helps us connect with the Divine. How does your own experience of religion measure up against these criteria?

- ✢ I also suggested that the presence of love in relationships is one of the best markers of healthy spirituality and that this love always involves a love of life. What is the overall quality of your relationship to others and to life itself? How do these relationships measure up against the criterion of love? How nurturing of such a posture of loving openness to others and to life itself is your spirituality?

- ✢ Another marker of healthy spirituality is an abiding sense of belonging in life and in the world, a feeling that is based on a sense of safety and trust. How solid is your sense of safety and belonging in the world? How does your spirituality relate to this?

- ✢ The third criterion of healthy spirituality is the robust sense of transcendent meaning that it should provide. What makes your life meaningful? How well does this framework do in terms of making suffering sufferable? How has your sense of personal meaning changed over the past decade?

One final and very important characteristic of healthy spirituality relates to the way in which it must be embodied. This is important enough that I will devote the entire next chapter to it.

7

Embodied Spirituality

I have said very little up to this point about one crucial component of the self—the body. It is time to do so because, apart from the body, concepts such as spirit, soul, and self remain too ethereal to be relevant to our lives. This is particularly true of spirituality, which, if it is not embodied, is escapist and dangerous. If the spiritual journey is to be grounded in the human journey, it must first be grounded in the body, for this is the primary home of self.

The Body Self

It is almost impossible for adults to reconnect to the primal awareness that was ours as young children—namely, that we are our bodies. Freud described the ego as a body ego, noting that our sense of self, before it becomes a mental abstraction, is always rooted in our bodies.[1] For infants, skin is the primary sensory organ, and the stimulation that it receives in feeding and holding is the core of our earliest experience as humans. Later—but still before our identification with our thoughts—muscles will serve this same role as our primary sensory organ and the focus of our experience. If as adults we are tempted to believe "I think, therefore I am," the infant's experience would clearly be "I feel, therefore I am." For the infant, all feeling is body feeling, all knowing is body knowing, and all consciousness is body consciousness.

Our alienation from our bodies as adults is so thorough that rather than thinking of our self as *being* our body we have come to believe that we *have* a body. Often we do not like the body we happen to have, and so we do things—surgical and otherwise—to change it and make it into something closer to our ideal body self. But, rather than improving our relationship to our bodies, this just increases the distance between us and our actual somatic self. Alienation from our bodies lies at the core of our alienation from our deepest self and from the world. Until we can be at home in our bodies, we can never truly be at home anywhere. Until we can return to being grounded in our self as a biological organism, we will be forever vulnerable to looking for substitute anchors for our being.

One such false anchor for the self is ideology. The person who is truly grounded in his or her body may support a cause, but if they do so it will not be to validate their existence. Life becomes its own meaning, and the person's existence is already solidly established. However, cut off from the root of life of our body, we inevitably seek meaning in other places. Beliefs become substitutes for somatic groundedness—as do things like possessions, prestige, influence, and image. But all prove somewhat unsatisfactory when spirit and soul are not securely rooted in our body.

It is probably fair to place much of the blame for the misunderstanding of our relationship to our bodies at the feet of Plato. Prior to him, the soul was regarded as the spirit of the body. Plato changed this metaphor, and the soul suddenly became the prisoner of the body. The destiny of the soul was, therefore, to leave the body and merge with the Godhead, for at death the body was understood as having served its humble purpose of transporting the precious inner spiritual cargo safely through life.

The human self will never have any real coherence unless we recognize that its roots are visceral. The self is an embodied self. It is incarnate—or in *caro*, which is Latin for "flesh." This word *caro* is a very un-Platonic word. There is nothing spiritual about it. It reminds us that we are creatures of flesh in all its raw, brute physicality.

Men are sometimes thought to be more in touch with the brute physicality of their body self than women. Men like the strength of their muscles. They like to play sports and do "man-ual" tasks. They like to push themselves to the limits of their endurance. They are, however, at least as alienated from their bodies as women, and probably more. When men try to whip their bodies into shape, often they are merely adding a superficial layer of pain to further insulate them from their deep body dis-ease. Commenting on professional football, James Nelson suggests that "for all its celebration of bodily toughness, it depends on dissociation from the body—not listening to its feelings of tiredness or pain or tenderness."[2] Most men are out of touch with their need for touch. They are cut off from the true strength that comes not from subduing the body but from aligning with it. Their attitude toward their bodies is more one of instrumentality than of cooperation. The body, therefore, is nothing more than something else to be conquered.

This state of being out of touch with their bodies blocks men's access to their feelings. It also impairs empathy toward others. Dissociation from the body and the emotions may be the root of the absence of moral sensitivity to the suffering men all too often inflict on themselves and others.[3] As men who batter others give ample testimony, those who are unable to feel their own pain are more likely to inflict pain on others. Our body is our link to the world, and when we no longer experience pain we lose touch with both internal and external reality.

But it is certainly not just men who have a disordered relationship with their body self. Women's relationships with their bodies often get distorted in different ways than men's, but the underlying alienation from their somatic self is at least as serious. Eating disorders are approximately ten times more common in women than in men. Anorexia—the disorder with the most profound disturbance in body image and involving the most marked dissociation from the body self—is approximately twenty times more common in females than in males. Likewise, dieting and weight preoccupation, as well as dissatisfaction with one's body, all occur significantly more often in women than in men.

Primal Alienation

Obviously there are numerous factors involved in producing these forms of alienation from our bodies. Sociocultural considerations get most of the popular attention at the moment, particularly in relation to disturbances experienced by women. But the most important source of this alienation from our bodies lies much deeper, in the same soil where we discovered the roots of our egocentricity—early wounds to our sense of well-being resulting from the inevitable experience of the person who was closest to us (usually our mother) failing to move in harmony with our needs. She may have been absent when we felt we needed her, or present but failed to give us what we felt we most needed. One way or another, a mismatch occurred. And then it occurred again, and again. The result was that suddenly our sense of fit within the world took a serious blow.

The disjunction of self that comes from this is the primal narcissistic injury that lies beneath both our egocentricity and our alienation from our bodies. As we saw earlier, egocentricity is our defense against further damage. But beyond this, it also distracts us from the painful inner abyss that now lies on the fault line between body and self. This abyss is our alienation from our bodies. With each experience of this mismatch between our self and our world, the abyss opens up further and our alienation from our bodies increases. Let me explain how this happens.

Our first awareness of the mismatch between the movement of our primary caretaker and our needs is our first experience of consciousness. It is an awareness of our self as separate from other realities that are not-self. Consciousness arises, therefore, with the onset of our awareness that we are not at one with all that is. But even more important is the fact that this is our first experience of being an object. Prior to this, we looked into our mother's eyes and saw ourselves reflected back. The self we were coming to know was, therefore, the self-in-relationship—our self as one-with-mother. We came to know this self by looking into the mirror of our mother's face. What we saw in this mirror changed, however, when we first became aware that mother was not an extension of our self that acted mechanically in response to our inner needs and desires. What we began to see from that point forward was mother as a separate self.

This moment marks the birth of our identity as a separate being in the world. But it also marks the birth of our alienation from our bodies. The distinction between self and others introduced a shift from self as subject to self as object. Along with the dawning sense of separateness came an emerging shift from an authentic inner focus to a more social exterior focus. Suddenly we were not only aware of the fact that others existed but, more crucially, we realized that we were simply an other for those others.[4] And slowly we were drawn away from the subjective experience of our self in our body to an objective view of our self as seen by others. Not only is this a shift from the subjective to the objective and from the inner to the outer, it is also a shift from the kinesthetic to the visual. Suddenly, the primary sense through which we knew our self and the world shifted from the felt experience of the body self to the visualization of the separate self as experienced by others. Over time we will pay an enormous price for this trade-off as it is the beginning of our movement from our senses to our thoughts. It also represents the movement from our immediate and lived self to a socially constructed self—something that can be seen by others and that allows us to be seen in a chosen light. It also, therefore, represents the beginning of a drift from the life of an authentic self to the life of the false self.

This is our inner abyss. It is our primal alienation. Most people go through their life with only limited awareness of this emptiness and disjunction. However, our restlessness and dis-ease betray a nagging sense of having been displaced from Eden and of no longer being able to remember the route back home. While it is common to think about this in existential or spiritual terms, it is important to recognize that the roots of this dis-ease are both somatic and spiritual. We are out of touch with both our bodies and the transcendent. Both are part of the ground of our being. Feeling at home anywhere starts with feeling at home in our bodies.

The Emotional Self

It would take me too far from my intended focus to offer a careful consideration of the effect these shifts away from the body have on the emotions, but I do want to say something about the relationship of emotions to our body self. Most of us realize that emotions are closer to the body than thoughts. This is one reason they are often not trusted and are incorrectly thought to be the enemies of good judgment.[5] Sometimes they feel like tsunamis of the psyche, appearing out of nowhere without warning and throwing our well-being and equilibrium into chaos. Is it any wonder then that so many people try to shut down their emotions and consequently further lose contact with their bodies?

Emotions present us with a crucial connection between mind and body. They are the brain's representations of body states. Just as objects in the external world cause patterns of activation of sensory receptive cells that we experience as sensory perceptions, so too do activation patterns in the internal world result in body states that we experience as emotions. For example, if while you are out walking alone one dark night you suddenly encounter an aggressive-looking dog, you see the dog (resulting from activation of visual receptive cells) but you feel fear (resulting from sympathetic nervous system activation that alters the body's internal state). Emotions are, therefore, a way of monitoring what is happening in our bodies. In fact, they are part of a homeostatic mechanism by which the brain keeps our internal environment in balance.

Our emotions and senses offer us crucial ways of remaining in contact with our bodies. This is why body and experiential psychotherapies try to help people get out of their minds and into their senses. And it is why the body, the senses, and the emotions all have a crucial role to play in spirituality. I will explore this further in later chapters where we will consider a number of practical things we can do to open up our senses, embrace our emotional realities, and attend to what is going on in our bodies.

But there is an even more obvious and powerful connection with our bodies that remains present for most people, regardless of how out of touch we may be with our somatic self: our sexuality. Here especially we will see crucial ways in which this dimension of our body experience connects with spirituality.

Our Sexual Self

Nothing has quite the power of sexuality to either integrate or fragment life. The Latin root of our English word *sex—secare*—means "to cut off" or "sever" and reminds us of this potential for disintegration. To be sexed is to be cut off from the whole. Most of us experience gender identification with only half the human population and recognize ourselves as unlike the other half in important ways. At some level of consciousness we are aware that we and our gender tribe represent only part of a larger human community. The incompleteness we feel in sexuality is comparable to the separated white and yolk of an egg. Together they make a whole; apart they are incomplete. The sexes are like that. "Alone we are essentially incomplete and aching at every level for a wholeness that unconsciously we know is not ours. We experience ourselves as white or yolk, separated from the other half."[6]

But notice that while the fact of being gendered involves separation, at the same time it points us back in the direction of wholeness. Sexuality orients us to the other, making us aware that our own wholeness is dependent on relationship with others. Gendered relational dynamics enrich human affairs and attract us to those who seem to hold the fulfillment of our longing for intimacy and wholeness. That fulfillment and wholeness involves more than finding a lover, because our sexuality involves more than having sex. It even involves more than finding a soul mate, because the wholeness that our sexuality points us toward is bigger than interpersonal connectedness. Each of these things forms a part of sexuality, but just a part.

Sexuality is the all-encompassing energy that is life itself. It reflects the fact that we are wired for love, intimacy, and relationship. It is life surging within us and propelling us in the direction of not only love, friendship, family, and community but also generativity, delight, ecstasy, humor, union, and self-transcendence. It is an ever-present inner call to high-octane, passionate life—life that is lived not just in bed but also at work and in all our relationships. Every part of life should be enriched by our sexuality. As important as the genitals are to sexuality, genital stimulation and orgasm form only one part of its larger reality.

For those who are sexually active, as well as for those who by choice or circumstances are not, sexuality is the call to engagement and vital relationship. I know people who are living a celibate lifestyle but are much more sexually alive than others who are genitally promiscuous. Every human relationship is enriched by the presence of sexuality. The dynamics of sexual interest and attraction add zest to relationships. The gendering of humans makes people more interesting. To deny this attraction forces unacceptable sexual urges to take on a life of their own in the unconscious, making them much more likely to be expressed in inappropriate ways. But to those who embrace their sexuality and allow it to take its place within the rest of personhood, it enriches life and makes interpersonal relationships more whole.

Integrated Sexuality

The journey toward integration is never linear, and the destination is always elusive. Integration is nonetheless a worthy goal. Sometimes a movement toward a deeper integration requires that we be willing to pass through a period of disintegration. Often this is associated with the collapse of life postures that are based in denial and falsity rather than in the cold, hard truths of reality. When these implode, as they inevitably will, we suddenly find ourselves in free fall as we lose our grounding in everything that previously held us and tumble into an unknown chasm of darkness. But ultimately that disintegration is always in the service of a deeper movement toward wholeness.

Our sexuality is intimately tied up with this movement toward wholeness. That is why, when it is properly embraced and channeled, sexuality holds unique potential as a source of integration. Because it emerges from the meeting place of body, spirit, and soul it uniquely draws its energy from each and, at its best, weaves all the disparate parts of self together.[7]

The foundation of sexuality is obviously biological. At an organic level we are gendered as either male or female, and usually, although not always, this is quite unambiguous. The focus at the level of this organic foundation is on having sex—sexual stimulation, sexual intercourse, sexual orgasm. Desire is not directed toward the other as a person but toward the other as a potential source of gratification. Desire at this level is physical, raw, and simple. It says, "I am sexually aroused. I want sexual gratification, and I want it now." It speaks in what Freud called *primary process language*.

Soul offers a broader horizon for the sexuality that emerges from this somatic foundation. Here sexuality is gendered to one degree or another as either masculine or feminine by both physiological differences and social conditioning. The focus at the level of soul is the expression and actualization of such things as love, romance, deep connection, emotional bonding, and ecstasy. Soul reaches out for loving relatedness and expresses this desire not simply in having sex but in making love. The voice of the soul might be heard as saying something like, "I want you. I love you. I desire you." Much more relational than simply mechanical or biological, the soul speaks in what Freud called *secondary process language*. It honors the separateness of the other but desires togetherness.

Spirit offers an even larger horizon for sexuality. At this level we are not gendered; spirit is identical in all humans. But while there is nothing sexual about human spirit itself, spirituality is a way of living that very much involves sexuality. The thrust of spirit is toward integration and wholeness through self-transcendence. Its voice speaks less of ephemeral desire than of deep longing. It speaks through our yearning for union and surrender that will overcome our alienation and separateness. It is built on self-transcending openness to all reality. It is concerned with "knowing, loving, and caring, and through interpersonal sharing of beliefs and values, results in communion, family, culture."[8] It shares the relational focus of soul but seeks relationship with the Beyond that is met in the other. The voice of spirit may be heard passionately crying, "I cherish you! I care for you! I long to truly know you!" Freud had no category to account for this language of spirit.

Sexuality and Spirituality

Sexuality is inextricably connected to spirituality because it involves our deepest sources of vitality, shapes our lived meaning, and holds unique potential to support the integration of personhood. The flow of all sexual energies is toward the harmonious alignment of body, soul, and spirit. The central agenda of sexuality is to channel in one direction our body's vitality and responses, our affections, and our caring. When this occurs, the person one truly cherishes and cares for will be the person one loves, and this will also be the person who arouses one's sexual response and physical desire.[9] Human love is then integrated; body, spirit, and soul are then aligned.

Sex becomes spiritual not by praying before making love (and then trying not to enjoy it too much!), but by embracing and then channeling our sexual passions in ways that support vital living and integration of personhood. Sex is spiritual because of the potential it has to bring fun, playfulness, attraction, charm, romance, vivaciousness, intensity, presence, spontaneity, and freedom into our lives. It is spiritual because of the way it can uniquely lead us out of self-centered isolation toward togetherness and community.

The healing, restorative, and integrative nature of sexuality is apparent even when we look at it exclusively at the level of bodily response. The experience of sexual arousal and orgasm makes an unquestionable contribution to physical well-being. It reduces stress, relaxes and calms the body, and opens access to a whole range of psychic material that often flows into consciousness because of the release of control that is part of orgasm. That release of control is itself an enormous gift, something many uptight people could immensely benefit from if they experienced it more regularly. In order for orgasm to happen, you must be prepared to move out of your head and into your body. The deepest sexual pleasure does not come from grasping but from releasing. If we are able to learn from them, our bodies are ready to teach us this extremely important spiritual truth.

Sexuality pulls us beyond our isolated individual self toward others. Though sex may be at times a solitary experience, even this is usually accompanied by fantasies of others. Sexuality is spiritual because it moves us toward love-shaped connections. In a sexual encounter we meet another in a deep, vulnerable, and potentially transformational place. The sharing and mutuality that exist in this place have as much potential as any spiritual practice to open us up to our depths and connect us to that which transcends our individual self.

For many, however—and for all of us at some points—sexuality is more associated with frustration and lack of fulfillment than with joy and bliss. Karl Rahner once said that "in the torment of the insufficiency of everything attainable we eventually realize that, here in this life, all symphonies remain unfinished."[10] While sexuality may represent a drive toward overcoming separateness, it often fails to accomplish this. People sleep alone who long for the comfort of another body and for the companionship of another soul. Others are victims of sexual abuse—a burden they carry in their bodies, spirits, and souls into every relationship, particularly every sexual encounter. Many are caught in the cul-de-sac of sexual addiction—compulsion replacing freedom, and genuine fulfillment being more elusive than ever. To these and many more, sexuality does not seem like a blessing. It brings pain, not bliss. It does not seem in any way to be a dynamic of life and integration. And if it is viewed as spiritual, it feels like a dark demonic presence.

Aloneness and togetherness are inseparable in sexuality.[11] We all sleep alone, whether we are having sex or not, because we are all caught in the existential and somatic reality of being isolated in the separateness of our individual bodies. How we relate to our loneliness will determine how deeply we meet another in the moments of togetherness. In the absence of sufficient aloneness, we fail to adequately appreciate the separateness of the other. But when we are prepared to lean into our aloneness with gentle acceptance, then it is possible to also lean deeply into the opportunities for togetherness that exist. Often the brokenness of sexual union results from turning away from one's own aloneness into another. This reduces the possibility of sex leading to genuine sexual encounter. The healing aspects of sexual encounter flow when we are able to befriend our aloneness and bring it—along with all the rest of us—to the other. This then allows sex to blossom into authentic sexual union.

But there is another reason sexuality is closely connected to loneliness. Human sexual longing is the expression of spirit, not just body. It is our reaching out to touch and to be held by the Infinite. This means that ultimately no finite other can fill all the yearning that is part of our sexuality. We are all yearning to surrender body, soul, and spirit not just to an other but to the Wholly Other. In the words of Thomas Moore, "Part of the pain of love is that no person, however suitable and satisfying, completes the desire for love. There is always a remainder because love takes us beyond the human sphere. It puts you in touch with the ultimate object of desire."[12]

The Religious Context of Sexuality

Talk of ultimate objects of desire and the Wholly Other brings us back to the realm of religious spirituality. Quite obviously, religion has not always been very affirming of the place sexuality has in spirituality. Paul Ricoeur describes three stages in the Western understanding of the relationship between the two.[13] The earliest stage closely identified spirituality and sexuality, giving sexuality a rich place in religious myth and ritual. This was followed by a second stage that entailed a dramatic separation of the two spheres: the sacred became increasingly transcendent while sexuality was demythologized and its power feared and constrained. Ricoeur notes, however, that there now seems to be an emerging third stage, marked by a desire to reconnect sexuality and the experience of the sacred, thus returning sexuality to its natural home within spirituality.

If such a shift is happening, it is possible because of the development of a holistic understanding of persons that allows us to see the ways in which sexuality is present in all human experience. Sexuality is so much more than specific behaviors. It is a sacred energy flowing through every cell of our being that calls us out of our isolation and loneliness into communion and community. It is the impulse to celebrate, to be creative, and to live with passion and generativity. It is saying YES! to life.

In sharp contrast to how it is often viewed, sexuality is neither incidental nor detrimental to our experience of the Divine. It is no coincidence that mystics—Christian and non-Christian alike—often use sexual imagery to describe union with God. Ann and Barry Ulinov remind us that "the language of sexual intimacy is the only fitting way

to give words to the experience of the unspeakable joy of that purifica-
tion, illumination, and movement toward union that we call the mystic
way."[14] The Song of Solomon (or Song of Songs) is so full of sexual
language that it leaves some Christians blushing and bewildered about
why it is included in the Bible. Christian mystical theology affirms that
sexuality points us beyond human communion and intimacy to the
ultimate fulfillment that we can have in union with God.

The mystical traditions of Islam present a very similar picture of
our ultimate fulfillment. Both Hafiz (the fourteenth-century Sufi mystic and much-loved Iranian poet) and Rumi (his Turkish counterpart
from a century later) wrote volumes of love poems to and about God
that were filled with passion and sexual imagery. Listen to the short
poem "You Better Start Kissing Me" by Hafiz.

> Throw away
> All your begging bowls at God's door,
> For I have heard the Beloved
> Prefers sweet threatening shouts,
> Something in the order of:
> "Hey, Beloved,
> My heart is a raging volcano
> Of love for you!
> You better start kissing me—
> Or Else!"[15]

The Sufis have a strong sense of the union with God that is love.
They teach that love is the way in which the ego is dethroned and the
illusion of our separateness overcome. They understand that our
sexuality ultimately points us toward these deepest desires, and they
ground their spirituality in the body. In fact, Thomas Merton, undoubtedly the best known twentieth-century Christian mystic, was a
great admirer of Sufi spirituality for exactly this reason. He honored
the Sufi tradition of the whirling dervish because he recognized in it
what he described as the purest form of meditation that existed—pure
because it is free of thought and grounded in the body.

Being an Embodied Self

We are, as I have been arguing, our bodies. But we are more than our
bodies. Because our bodies represent our most visible identity, it is

easy for us to equate our self with our bodies. But equating our self with a body that is destined to dysfunction, decline, and decay always leads to suffering. If you are your body, when beauty fades and vigor diminishes, you fade and diminish. But in reality, it is in those periods of the ebbing of our physical self that we are often most able to experience the strength of spirit and soul that makes us most distinctively human. I have learned this not from books but from my own journey through the late decades of the middle passage of life.

And so, paradoxically, we must ground our self in our body but must not limit our self to it. The equation of our self with our body is one of the fundamental illusions that deep spirituality warns us against. Ultimately, to discover my truest and deepest self I must move beyond my body, even beyond what I experience as my individual self. I must discover a new sense of "I"—a knowing of me that comes from finding myself in a larger whole. This is the spiritual route to our true self. In it, my self and the other are finally understood to be interrelated aspects of something larger—of God.

Teilhard de Chardin suggests that the prevailing contemporary view is that the body is "a fragment of the Universe, a piece completely detached from the rest and handed over to a spirit that informs it. In the future we shall have to say that . . . my matter is not a part of the Universe that I possess *totaliter*: it is the totality of the Universe possessed by me *partiliter*."[16] Both our materiality and our deepest self participate in the stuff of all that is. However, limited by our egocentric ways of knowing and being, we fail to be aware of this truth.

Grounding Spirituality in the Body

Once again, let me suggest taking a moment to reflect on what it means to be an embodied self.

- How open, deep, and vital is your connection with your body, your emotions, and your sexuality? When you consider the central role that the body should play in a truly life-enhancing spirituality, how do you assess the health of your spiritual life?
- What false anchors for your identity might be present if your self is not grounded in your body? The text mentions such things as ideology, possessions, reputation, and image, but many oth-

ers also exist. If your attachment to your body is weak, what grounds your self and keeps you connected to the world?

- ✛ How integral is your sexuality to your life? How does your spirituality either help or hinder this? To what extent does your sexuality vitalize and empower the passions that are most central to your spirituality and to your life? What are the respective contributions of body, soul, and spirit to your sexuality and spirituality?

- ✛ How does being embodied contribute to your participation in the stuff of all that is? What, if anything, do you know of yourself as the totality of the universe possessed partially by you?

Deep spirituality teaches that we are all spiritually blind—unaware of the deepest realities that surround us. Like the fish in the Sufi story who swim around feverishly searching for the sea, we need to have our eyes opened to the truth that what we seek we are already within. As described by Saint Paul, it is knowing that in Christ "we live, and move, and exist" (Acts 17:28). The spiritual life starts with awareness. This is the foundation of the soulful spiritual practices that we will examine in part 3 of the book, and so it is the one we begin with in the next chapter.

PART THREE

Spiritual Practices for the Human Journey

8

Awareness

The story is told of an apprentice to the famous Zen master Nan-in who, after completing ten years of training, went to visit his master one rainy day. As he entered the room, Nan-in greeted him with a question: "Did you leave your sandals and umbrella on the porch?" "Yes," the apprentice answered. The master continued, "Did you place your umbrella to the right of your sandals or to the left?" "To the right," the apprentice answered confidently, rather pleased with himself. "And, were you breathing in or out when you slipped off your left sandal?" Not knowing the answer, the apprentice realized at once that he had not yet attained full awareness and immediately extended his apprenticeship.

This story might strike you as ridiculous. But if it does it may be because you have not yet realized either the importance or the difficulty of living with awareness.

Parables about the importance of being aware and awake are common across human cultures and spiritual traditions. Being blind and coming to see, being asleep or dead and coming to life, living in a state of unconsciousness or delusion and coming to truth and reality—in whatever form they are presented, these stories tell us that the transformation of consciousness is radical but that it is fundamental to the spiritual journey.

The spiritual life starts with awareness. Limited awareness equates to a shallow spiritual life. No one can ever be more aware of the self-transcendent than they are aware of things going on within and around them. The spiritual journey starts, therefore, with awakening—and with being prepared to awake again and again as we realize that we have once again drifted into sleep.

The truth is that we all go through most of life as sleepwalkers. We need to awaken and learn to see. Spirituality is about seeing and being awake. In Sanskrit, *Buddha* means "the awakened one," and awakening from the womb of sleep is the central goal of Buddhism.[1] It is said that soon after his enlightenment, the Buddha passed a man on a road who, noting the peacefulness of his presence, asked if he was a god. The Buddha said he was not a god. The man then asked if he was a magician or wizard. Again, he said he was not. When then asked what he was, the Buddha answered, "I am awake."[2] In Sufism, awakening is also right at the heart of the spiritual journey and is understood as learning to see all things through the eyes of God.[3]

Awakening is equally important in Christianity. The Bible is full of encouragements to look, see, listen, heed, and attend. We are urged to rise from our sleep, listen to what the Spirit is saying, and pay attention so that we may notice that God is already paying attention to us (see Pss. 5:3; 33:18; Rom. 13:11; Rev. 2:7). Jesus often taught his followers about the importance of staying watchful and awake (Matt. 25:13; Luke 12:37). He reserved his harshest criticism for religious leaders who thought they could see but in fact were blind. He called them fools and warned of the enormous danger both to them and to others as they blindly led people to the edge of a pit into which they both would inevitably fall (Matt. 15:14). He taught that when our spiritual eyes are healthy and discerning, our whole body is full of light (Luke 11:34). And he used the most radical of all possible words to describe this ascent from unconsciousness and sleepwalking. He described this awakening as being born again (John 3:3–8 NASB).

Awareness is not just important for the life of the spirit. It is equally foundational to the life of the soul. Mary Oliver notes that the soul is built entirely out of attentiveness.[4] Attentiveness allows us to live in places of depth where life can become its own meaning. Inattentiveness, on the other hand, dooms us to live in shallow places that deprive the soul of the essential ingredient that it needs to thrive: contact with reality. When we fail to pay attention, we inevitably end up living soullessly.

George Gurdjieff, a popular twentieth-century Armenian mystic and spiritual teacher, said that the fundamental human problem is that we keep falling asleep.[5] We may awaken for brief moments of intense emotional experience, but then we quickly slip back into a tangled dream of neurotic fantasy. Most of the time we live as mindless robots. The invitation of soulful spirituality is to awaken, to respond rather than simply react, and to become full participants in our lives.

Learning to Pay Attention

Typing the phrase "pay attention" just now immediately takes me back to the innumerable times when, as a child, I was told to do exactly this by my parents and teachers. This would happen when I was caught up in some interior world of imagination or preoccupation and was not sufficiently heedful of what was being said to me. However, the kind of attention that spirit and soul require is quite different from this effortful focusing of our thoughts and constriction of our imagination. In many ways it is the exact opposite. Paying attention as a practice of soulful spirituality is not scrunching up your willpower and tightening your focus but simply opening yourself to what you encounter. This makes it much more an act of release than an act of effort. What we release is any attempt to control attention; instead, we allow it to be absorbed by our present experience.

This sort of attentive awareness is sometimes described as contemplation. Contemplation is an apprehension of existence that is wide awake and uncluttered by thought. Suppose you are standing on the edge of a deciduous forest in spring and suddenly notice the variety of shades of green in front of you. Contemplative knowing of that sea of variegated green is simply allowing your attention to be absorbed by it—being fully present to it, not simply to your thoughts about it.

Simone Weil built her short life of thirty-four years around the constant practice of this sort of attention. She described it as detaching from her thoughts and leaving her awareness empty and ready to be penetrated by whatever she encountered.[6] Attention, she argued, is the best preparation for prayer, and absolutely unmixed attention is prayer.[7] It is a state of active receptivity that opens us up to the sacred. This is exactly how the contemporary Quaker author Douglas Steere understands prayer, describing it as "awakeness, attention, intense inward openness." Sin, in his view, is anything that destroys this attentiveness.[8]

The greatest threat to attention is thought. Thinking is a siren on the rocky coast, calling to spirit as it soars in the wind. It is seductively attractive because it seems so benign, so familiar. But thinking about experience removes us from it. It places us above it, outside it. The gap between perception and interpretation is the place where we lose awareness and slip into unconscious living. This is also the place where joy, creativity, and aliveness are lost. Instead of thinking about what we are experiencing and trying to analyze or understand it, contemplative awareness involves simply allowing our selves to be captivated by it. Rather than us trying to get *it*, we allow it to get *us*.

Thinking is not in itself the problem. It is a distinctively human capacity and an enormously important part of what it means to be human. However, if we are not aware of the way in which it draws us away from openness to the present moment into a place of preoccupation, we will forever be its slave. Like so many things, thinking is a valuable servant but a terrible master.

Describing this act of paying attention as contemplation may make it seem too esoteric to be practical, something for spiritual elites but not simple enough to be useful to the rest of us. However, far from being an advanced state of consciousness, contemplation is simple, pure, and natural. This sort of paying attention is something at which young children excel. Their capacity to be absorbed by a single thing is immense. Imagine, for example, the young child engrossed with a snail, or ripples on a puddle, or the texture of the food he or she is fingering instead of eating. This is precisely why children are so often told to "pay attention." They are, in fact, paying keen attention to something. It is simply not the thing to which the adult wishes them to attend, at least not at that moment.

There is a very important operating principle of spirit and soul at work here. Careful attention paid to anything is a doorway to the self-transcendent. Regardless of how insignificant the object may seem, being truly aware of it has enormous potential for growth of spirit and soul.

Take a moment and try the following simple exercise: Select a small object. It may be something manufactured (perhaps a pencil or a key) or something natural (maybe a small stone or a leaf). It does not matter what it is. What matters is how you attend to it. As soon as you finish reading this paragraph, put the book down and spend the next minute giving this object as much undivided attention as you can. Feel it, smell it, and look at it from as many angles as possible. Notice how heavy or light it is, how hard or soft. Don't analyze it as a scientist. Just allow it to capture your interest and hold your attention. Gaze at it in wonder and curiosity, and allow yourself to see it as if for the very first time.

Let's now talk about your experience. Perhaps you found your mind wandering and the task trivial or boring. Or maybe you found yourself quite engrossed with whatever you were holding in your hands. Regardless, if you spent the moment open to and engaged with whatever you were holding, you are now more aware than you were two minutes ago. Success in matters of spirit and soul is not nearly as important as intention. Paying attention to anything always succeeds in making us more awake.

Attending to the details of experience has enormous potential to enrich our spiritual journey. Unfortunately, most people live mindlessly, held in oblivion by their preoccupations. If this is you, the most life-giving spiritual practice for the next while may be taking a few minutes of stillness each day to pay attention to what is happening in and around you. Paying attention is the foundation of living spiritually and mindfully.

Mindfulness

Mindfulness is a spiritual practice that is most commonly associated with Buddhism, but it is also deeply congruent with Christianity, as well as any spirituality that prizes awareness. Its goal is to help us get off autopilot and actually live our lives rather than unconsciously flow down the stream of life. We can most simply define mindfulness as being aware and awake in the present moment. It is recognizing that we have once again fallen asleep but that we have a choice about whether we stay there. The choice we have is awareness.

Mindfulness, like contemplation, is neither complicated nor hard. The only difficulty is remembering to do it. All it requires is the simple act of noticing. Notice, for example, what is happening in your body right now. You might become aware of a stiff back. Or possibly you notice a slight headache or tension in your shoulders. Pay attention to whatever it is that comes into your awareness. This is a first step toward leaving your mind and coming to your senses. It is the first step toward awakening.

For most of us, there is a strong tendency to get lost in our thoughts and feelings. Both are important, but either can easily make us oblivious to what is happening in and around us. Our inner mental and emotional experiences keep us self-preoccupied and block us from genuine awareness. Notice, for example, what changes when you name your thoughts or feelings rather than just spinning or massaging them. Say to yourself, for example, "Now I am thinking about making dinner," or, "Now I am feeling anxious." As soon as you do so you will likely notice some distance from your thoughts and feelings. You might begin to realize that they are just the things that pass through your mind, things that float down the stream of your consciousness. They are not you, and they do not have any concrete reality or absolute truth. You can hold them or release them. But for now, just notice them. This is being mindful. Mindfulness isn't eliminating thoughts and feelings. It is being aware of your experience.

Because we are so prone to slipping into the oblivion of inner pre-occupation, it might be helpful if someone were with us throughout our day, periodically reminding us to wake up and be present to ourselves and to what is happening around us. Lacking this, mindfulness teachers often encourage students to treat environmental cues that arise in, or can be programmed into, the flow of one's day as such reminders—things like crossing the thresholds of doors or coming to red lights at traffic intersections or hearing hourly signals from watches or cell phones. The actual act of mindfulness at such points of reminder can be as simple as quickly noticing what is happening in your body. Or it might be paying attention to several successive breaths. Simply observe whatever you notice. This is the practice of mindfulness in its simplest form.

At a Buddhist retreat this reminder may come in the form of a bell that is rung—or possibly a Tibetan prayer bowl that is rubbed until it begins to make its distinctive sound. This is strikingly similar to the ancient Christian practice of stopping for a moment of prayerful stillness when the Angelus bells of the church rang at 6:00 a.m., noon, and 6:00 p.m. each day. It is also similar to the role of the public call to prayer in Muslim cities, where one may go to the mosque but will more often simply respond in a moment of prayerful awareness. Monastic life in many spiritual traditions is still organized around the periodic ringing of bells, which serves as an invitation to return to awareness, sometimes recognized as prayer.

But this sort of mindfulness is not just for monks. Writing to Christian laity, not simply clerics, Saint Benedict begins his book of spiritual precepts for those who seek to follow Christ with the words, "Let us arise. . . . Let us open our eyes to the deifying light, let us hear with attentive ears."[9] What he then went on to outline was a framework for awakening and being attentive to God throughout the day, organizing the day around what he described as the Divine Hours. These "hours" were times during the day (he recommended eight, and this was the pattern that became central to Western Christian monasticism) when Christians were encouraged to stop for a moment of prayerful stillness before God and God's Word. Christian monks and clergy may follow this pattern of regular daily breaks for time with God most faithfully, but the advice of Saint Benedict has also been warmly received by Christian laity over the centuries who wish to cultivate a habit of increased attentiveness to their mindful God.

The Present Moment

A crucial feature of mindful attentiveness is that it is anchored in the present moment. We can't pay attention to something in the past. We can remember it, but we cannot be mindful of it. You can only be mindful of something that is in the present. Consequently, paying attention is always an engagement with the now.

Suppose you are walking in a park. Paying attention is simply inviting yourself to be present to this experience and gently returning to the present each time you notice that you have gone somewhere else. As soon as you extend this invitation to yourself and notice what happens, it will be clear just how little time we actually spend in the present. Your body may well be walking in the park, but there is an excellent chance that your mind is somewhere else—either in the past or in the future. Most of us are easily seduced away from the present by obsessive remembering of that which has gone before and anxious anticipation of that which is still to come. And yet, the only place where we can ever actually be present is the now. Cultivation of the ability to live in the present moment is, therefore, the core of attentiveness.

The present moment is the ground on which life is lived. It cannot happen anywhere else. The only route to being fully alive entails being prepared to embrace the now. Not liking something about present reality does not change what is. Peace comes only from being one with life and one with the now. Eckhart Tolle notes that the ego thrives on the resentment of reality.[10] This is a very important observation. The more we pick and choose which aspects of reality we accept, the more we live in opposition to life itself. This is the life of the ego. But our larger and truer self recognizes the illusion that we can never control life and invites us to a relationship of acceptance of what is, as it is. The Buddhist word for reality is *tatata*—the suchness of life. Acceptance of that suchness is essential if we are to be truly aware and awake. All avoidance of it forces us to live in a place of pretense, denial, and oblivion. And since recognition of that which is beyond awareness always represents awakening, noticing how little time we actually live in the present is itself an act of developing awareness and wakefulness.

Our relationship with the now will always shape every other relationship we have. A dysfunctional relationship with the present moment will be reflected in a dysfunctional relationship with our self, with others, with the world, and with life. But on the other hand, an embrace of the present moment opens us up to life and all we encounter.

Breath as the Meeting of Body, Spirit, and Soul

Recently I spent several months at a center for interreligious spiritual dialogue in Hong Kong. One of the people I met there was a Taoist professor from Zhejiang University in China by the name of Zhang Xin Zhang. Knowing only a little about Taoism, and that mostly from books, I was very happy for the chance to spend long hours of conversation with this most interesting new friend. Hearing him describe his meditation routine, I was struck by how important paying attention to his breath was to his practice. More striking was his surprise that I, as a Christian, did not make this a central part of my own spiritual practice. He asked, "Am I not right that Christians understand their origins to lie in the infusion of divine breath into the dust of the earth?" I assured him that he was correct. "And," he continued, "am I not right that you understand each breath to be a gift from God?" Again, I said he was. "And," he pushed on, "am I not right that you understand that the Spirit of God is with you, moment by moment, breath by breath?" Again, I agreed. "Then how do you fail to see," he asked, "the immense spiritual value in attending to those moment-by-moment expressions of the presence of God?" I was convinced, and I soon found ways to make this a regular part of my own practice.

The ancient Sanskrit word for breath is *atman*. It means the "in-dwelling God." As my Taoist friend pointed out, this understanding is at the core of Christian theology but is surprisingly absent from most Christian spiritual practice. It is, however, far from alien to it. Prayerfully making each breath an act of drawing God in and then breathing God out onto the world is an ancient Christian practice. Sometimes this has been called *breath communion* because, just as Christians open themselves to God through eating and drinking in the eucharistic communion, so too each breath provides an opportunity to receive God.

The practice of breath attentiveness is equally compatible with any spiritual tradition that values the expansion of awareness. Some people do this by counting breaths. Others simply notice each breath. Hindu yogis often practice slowing the breath, evening it, and reducing the amount of air required. A typical exercise calls for breathing so gently across goose down touching the nostrils that an observer cannot tell if breath is being drawn in or out. Other breath attentiveness exercises simply encourage a noticing of successive breaths, without attempting to change anything. This is quite different from deep breathing as a tool of relaxation or stress management. It is simply practice in attentiveness as a way of offering spirit and soul room for growth through expanded awareness.

As long as we are alive, our breathing remains a doorway to presence in the moment. To walk through that doorway, all we have to do is take notice of our breathing. Whenever we feel carried away by an emotion or distracted by thoughts, we can return to our breathing to collect and anchor our being. We can become aware of the flow of air coming in and going out of our nose. We can feel our chest rise and fall. We can listen to the sound of exhalation and inhalation. At any time, regardless of where we are or what we are doing, we can return to this foundation of our life. Conscious breathing is a valuable means of uniting body, spirit, and soul and bringing the energy of mindfulness into the present moment.

Breath is the meeting point of body, spirit, and soul. In many cultures it has traditionally been understood as the way the soul enters the body. But it is also closely related to spirit. One of the most ancient words for spirit is the Hebrew *ruach*, which is also translated as "breath" or "wind." Breathing is not simply something we do; it is something that flows through us—something we might think of as life, or possibly as the Spirit. Witnessing breath is a powerful way to increase awareness because it forces us into the present moment. To be conscious of your breathing is to be present and awake.

The Gifts of Presence

Let me address a question that may be forming for you. Perhaps paying all this attention to your self is beginning to sound overly narcissistic. Maybe you feel that the self-preoccupation that it appears to involve will draw you into yourself and away from others. Once again, however, just the opposite is true. Because paying attention always brings us back to the present, it is a powerful way of breaking through the preoccupations that block our presence to others. Remembering to be present while in the midst of a conversation with someone could not, therefore, be more appropriate.

Recent research has demonstrated that increasing our mindfulness increases our capacity for a more resonant and empathic connection with others.[11] Mindful awareness seems to make a difference even at the level of brain structure, promoting the development of neurological circuits that appear to be involved in aiding attunement to the intentions and experiences of others.[12] It is clear that being attentive to our self in the present moment enhances our attentiveness to the other. Psychoanalytic psychotherapists have long known this and have emphasized the importance in therapeutic listening of paying attention not only to the patient but also to one's own depths. They have understood that we are most open to another when we are also open to our own self. The hospitality we offer ourselves will inevitably determine the limits of the hospitality we are capable of offering others. Far from being antisocial or narcissistic, being present to one's self is the prerequisite to being available for genuine encounter with other people.

Being present also makes us more likely to notice the brushes with the transcendent that punctuate our lives. I am convinced that these brushes are much more common than we realize. The problem, again, is limited awareness. Somehow, that which is truly beyond us will, every now and then, break through our slumber and touch our soul in an unforgettable manner. It may be while watching a sunset or gazing into a starry sky. Or it might happen while tucking your child in at night, driving to work, or talking to a stranger. But somehow we know that we are part of something bigger than our self. We sense our relationship to that larger reality and feel the harmony of our place within it. We experience a sense of belonging—of everything belonging. Cynthia Bourgeault describes it as "something like sounding the note G on the piano and instantly hearing the D and the B that surround it and make it a chord."[13] This awareness is truly extrasensory. Our normal faculties cannot bring it to us. But we may, in stillness and openness, occasionally receive it as a gift.

Several things characterize these moments. They may not feel religious or even spiritual, and because of this, people who are seeking spiritual or religious experience often do not notice them. Sometimes they are accompanied by affective intensity that has often been called a "shudder of the soul." Other times they are so ordinary and subtle that they are easily overlooked. One of their most consistent features is that we almost always experience them as something that without question is outside and beyond our self. This generally has a humbling effect in that it relativizes the ego by confronting us with realities beyond our small ego-life. Rather than feeling larger and grander (an inflated ego), we feel more whole (an integrated ego).

Carl Jung called these experiences *numinous encounters* and made attending to them the primary focus of Jungian analysis. He argued that they hold unique potential for our healing and integration.[14] The reason they are so important is that they point the way to freedom from our existential and spiritual isolation. They point to the possibility that in the depths of body, spirit, and soul we are fundamentally one with the Spirit, one with all that is. They penetrate the optical delusion that our identification with our small ego-self represents. They give us a glimpse of the Divine and of the way in which our own being and the Divine are mysteriously interwoven.

Being Aware

The good news about awareness is that it is something you can start to practice right now.[15] In fact, there is no time other than the now

in which to do so. Here are four simple things that you can do if you
wish to become more aware.

⊹ Take a moment—now and several times a day—to simply note
what is happening in your body. Your awareness of other things
will never be greater than your awareness of what is happening
in your body. First, sit in stillness with your eyes shut (if you
are comfortable doing so) for a moment or two. Then, starting
with your head and face, slowly scan your body, noting whatever you become aware of—moving slowly down through your
shoulders, neck, upper arms, elbows, forearms, wrists, hands,
fingers, chest, stomach, hips, buttocks, genitals, legs, feet, and
toes. Carefully notice the sensations associated with each body
part. Get up slowly after you complete this exercise, retaining a
sense of your body. Doing this regularly will begin to strengthen
your relationship with your body and make you more aware of
what you are feeling and experiencing.

⊹ Take a few moments to focus on your breath. First, get comfortable, either sitting with your back straight against a firm chair
or lying on your back. Relax and watch yourself breathe. Don't
do anything to change how you breathe. Just notice what is
happening. Notice that breathing continues without you doing
anything, and just observe this. If you find that your mind has
wandered, simply bring it back and once again watch yourself
breathe. Don't waste any energy reprimanding yourself. Just
observe. Now, after doing this for a few moments, count each
new breath as you draw it in. Again, don't attempt to change
anything about your breathing. Just focus on it, counting each
inhalation. Once you get to ten, start over again. Do this for
several minutes and then get up, allowing your breathing to
continue unobserved.

⊹ Look around you wherever you are right now. Allow your eyes
to settle on whatever object comes into the center of your field
of vision, and then focus on whichever part of this object you
first notice—holding this focus for two complete breath cycles.
Then move your attention to another object, again focusing on
whichever part of it first captures your attention, holding this
for another two complete breath cycles. Take five minutes to
continue doing this, allowing your attention to be fully absorbed
by the things that surround you wherever you are. Do this once

or twice a day in the environment where you spend most of your daytime. Notice how it begins to enliven your awareness in this environment that you may have become insensitive to because of its familiarity.

✛ Finally, do the same thing in a less familiar environment. Enter this place with expectancy and slowly allow yourself to truly see it. Allow your eyes to move around, but still keep them on one thing at a time for two complete breath cycles. Draw in each breath deeply, allowing yourself to be filled with the sensations of this place—what you can see, what you can smell, and what you can feel on the surface of your skin. Open all your sensory channels, keeping them focused on one thing at a time as that one thing comes into the center of your visual field.

Awareness is the doorway to both the present moment and the transcendent. Learning to live with increased awareness is allowing your self to awaken and begin to unfold. It is learning to live with openness and presence. It is, therefore, the foundation of soulful spirituality.

9

Wonder

Awareness never travels alone. Once it arrives and finds a welcoming home in our soul, we discover that it has brought along other guests. Wonder is often among them.

Seldom will this be wonder's first visit. Wonder is the natural companion of children. For most of us it was, therefore, very much part of our way of experiencing the world when we were younger—when we still knew how to do one thing at a time and how to allow that one thing to absorb us. That knowing led us to places of enchantment with small and seemingly insignificant things. It also allowed us to make fascinating discoveries about the world that we never could have made apart from wonder. It did this because wonder is the spirit behind awareness that transforms paying attention from a discipline to one of life's great joys.

Seeing through eyes of wonder, children notice things that adults can no longer perceive. But sadly, the shelf life of wonder in most children is quite short. William Wordsworth makes this point eloquently in his poem "Intimations of Immortality from Recollections of Early Childhood."

> There was a time when meadow, grove and stream
> The earth and every common sight

To me did seem
Appareled in celestial light,
The glory and the freshness of a dream.

It is not now as it hath been of yore.
Turn whereso'ere I may,
By night or day,
The light which I have seen
I now can see no more.[1]

The diminishment of our natural capacity to see the truly wondrous and to dance in enthrallment with the world begins when wonder is replaced by rationality. This happens to all but those who are fortunate enough to be encouraged to maintain imagination, curiosity, and creativity. In them, the roots of wonder may grow deep enough that it will persist through life. Many of those people become artists and poets. It is from them that we can learn the most about wonder if we have lost this natural childhood gift and wish to recover it.

The Enchanted World

Sometimes when I speak to Christians about the importance of things like awareness and wonder, they tell me that this all sounds rather New Age. I do not share their worry about learning from other spiritual paths. Actually, I am quite thankful for the way in which New Age religionists are calling us back to the sacralization of the world. The fruit of the Enlightenment has been a boringly small world devoid of both mystery and the sacred. Science offered us a brave new world of wonder-full technologies and products but has not lived up to its promises. A world devoid of mystery turns out to be a world that is too small for the human spirit. This is why Albert Einstein said, "The most beautiful experience we can have is the mysterious. . . . Whoever does not know it and can no longer wonder, no longer marvel, is as good as dead, and his eyes are diminished."[2]

In his poem "God's Grandeur," Gerard Manley Hopkins described the world as "charged with the grandeur of God." Elizabeth Barrett Browning presented a very similar picture.

Earth's crammed with heaven,
And every common bush afire with God;

But only he who sees, takes off his shoes,
The rest sit round it and pluck blackberries.[3]

Although both Hopkins and Browning were Christians, this was not
the reason they were able to discern the grandeur and sacredness of
the world. They were able to discern these things because they had
learned to pay attention and welcome wonder. Hafiz saw the same
world through Sufi eyes and offered the poem "Today" in response.

I
Do not
Want to step so quickly
Over a beautiful line on God's palm
As I move through the earth's
Marketplace
Today.

I do not want to touch any object in this world
Without my eyes testifying to the truth
That everything is
My Beloved.

Something has happened
To my understanding of existence
That now makes my heart always full of wonder
And kindness.

I do not
Want to step so quickly
Over this sacred place on God's body
That is right beneath your
Own foot

As I
Dance with
Precious life
Today.[4]

Some frame of reference is necessary when responding to the truly
wondrous, and religion's comfort with mystery often makes it a natural
choice. Science can never provide a big enough horizon to truly ac-
commodate this openness to mystery. Einstein recognized this, stating

that the encounter with that which we cannot penetrate by reason or science and which is accessible to our minds in only the most veiled manner constitutes the essence of true religiosity. In this sense, he said, he was truly a religious man.[5] Many scientists share this religious commitment with Einstein—a commitment expressed not in dogma or identification with institutional religion but in openness to mystery that can never be eliminated by analysis or reason.

Wonder and Reverence

The great Jewish rabbi Abraham Joshua Heschel said that there are two possible ways of knowing and responding to the world: the way of reason and the way of wonder.[6] The way of reason seeks to eliminate mystery and bring the world under our control. The way of wonder accepts the mysteries of life and responds with something that is familiar to children but forgotten by most adults: awe.

Reason and wonder are not mutually exclusive—just distinct. In fact, we can quite easily use both faculties to encounter the world and, by so doing, know it in ways that neither alone makes possible. Whatever we approach on the basis of reason we attempt to tame and exploit, making it conform to our concepts and control. Our concepts then stand between us and everything else we encounter. But before we employ reason to try to conceptualize what we encounter, we experience amazement. If we retain this radical capacity for amazement, we may be able to sidestep the impulse to control what we encounter and instead submit to the truly amazing and adjust our concepts to it. Doing so is the prerequisite for any authentic awareness of that which is. Theories and explanations separate us from astonishment and close the doorway to mystery and the sacred. Only wonder allows us to be truly open to the world.

Knowing by the way of wonder gets *you*; you never simply get *it*. In the words of Rabbi Heschel, "The stirring in our hearts when watching the star-studded sky is something no language can declare. What smites us with unquenchable amazement is not that which we grasp and are able to convey but that which lies within our reach but beyond our grasp—the ineffable. Under the running sea of our theories and scientific explanations lies the aboriginal abyss of radical amazement."[7] The search for reason ends on the shore of the unknown. But the ineffable dwells in the immense expanse beyond it.

Wonder will only emerge in the presence of reverence. If nothing is sacred, nothing worthy of reverence, then nothing will evoke wonder. This is the plight of the cynic. Cynicism is the way we try to minimize the loss of wonder and idealism. It is the mask we hide behind when we choose to despise the simple and wondrous. Wonder may yet exist, but cynics will usually feel too vulnerable to dare to embrace it. Wonder demands openness, and that openness is simply too threatening for those who are cynical.

Reverence for life encourages openness and awe. It makes room for each person or thing to be encountered in their own uniqueness. When all of life is treated as sacred, it becomes possible then to experience it as sacred, and as this happens, wonder begins to burst upon us.

Befriending Mystery

The cultivation of attentiveness may give us a chance to welcome wonder back into our life, but wonder will not take root apart from openness to mystery. Mystery is the enemy of those with an insatiable need for explanation and control, but it is a friend to those living in the thrall of wonder. It is not a compromise of intellect to accept, even appreciate, mystery. The great mysteries of life—love, suffering, evil, death, beauty—do not need to be figured out in order to be engaged. But they must be befriended if the encounter is to be nurturing to spirit and soul. Any other attitude lacks the hospitality that transforms mystery from being the enemy to being a welcome companion on our human journey.

Mystery is much more than a knowledge gap—something as temporary as a question awaiting an answer. Mystery is not simply the not-yet-known. The great mysteries of human life are incapable of being solved or eliminated. We can know them existentially or contemplatively but not rationally. In other words, we can live them, but we cannot solve them. We can know them as part of the human condition without ever explaining them.

Contemplatives often speak of mystery as something that can be known (as in, befriended) without being known (as in, understood). Contemplative knowing is gentler than analytical knowing. It does not seek to annihilate but to offer hospitality. Listen to this posture of hospitality in another poem by William Wordsworth.

For I have learned
To look on nature, not as in the hour
Of thoughtless youth; but hearing often times
The still, sad music of humanity,
Nor harsh nor grating, though of ample power
To chasten and subdue. And I have felt
A presence that disturbs me with the joy
Of elevated thoughts; a sense sublime
Of something far more deeply interfused,
Whose dwelling is the light of setting suns,
And the round ocean and the living air,
And the blue sky, and in the mind of man:
A motion and a spirit, that impels
All thinking things, all objects of all thought,
And rolls through all things.[8]

Here we see welcoming attentiveness to the world and its mysteries, but without any need to either ignore or explain that which cannot be controlled or understood. This willing openness is at the core of contemplative living and is a life-giving part of soulful spirituality.

The unknown is our closest companion in the human journey. We may try to deny its presence in an arrogant pretense of being in control of our lives, but in reality, it is with us at every step. We face the unknown as we draw in each breath. The next moment can, and may, change our life. Many people live with a story organized around the two parts of their life—the dividing line between the two being a turning point that arose, unexpectedly and beyond their control, in an instant. Our future is unknown and our past filled with much more mystery than most of us ever care to acknowledge. We create stories in an effort to tame the unknowns of our past, but they simply stitch it together in a superficial way that never truly eliminates mystery.

Since ancient times, religion has been one of the ways humans have attempted to befriend the unknown. Because it provides a framework for remaining open to mystery, religion allows us to engage the unknown without needing to solve it. John O'Donohue points out that wonder in the face of mystery is a natural source of prayer.[9] It is prayer that allows us to respond to the unknown with wonder rather than fear.

Obviously, however, not all religious spirituality maintains openness to mystery. Rationalism, moralism, fundamentalism, legalism, and a great host of other isms easily strip a religious life posture of all the softness and flexibility that spirituality would otherwise produce. Mystery and wonder have a small place in such a life. Regardless of how much people under the pall of such isms may talk about worship, the god who is being worshiped has now been tamed into the image of its fervent followers, and genuine mystery, awe, and wonder will be very limited.

The Transformation of the Ordinary

But it is not just under conditions of constricted religious spiritual- ity that the transcendent fails to engender wonder. Most of us are blind to the wonder that lies hidden in the ordinary events of daily life, yet it is precisely in the ordinary that wonder can disclose the most splendor.

In one of her short stories, Jhumpa Lahiri eloquently describes this transformation of our ability to perceive the ordinary with wonder. Listen in as the narrator of the story sums up his life in London with the twelve penniless Bengali bachelors like himself who shared a small house and humble existence: "While the astronauts, heroes forever, spent mere hours on the moon, I have remained in this new world for nearly thirty years. I know that my achievement is quite ordinary. . . . Still, there are times I am bewildered by each mile I have traveled, each meal I have eaten, each person I have known, each room in which I have slept. As ordinary as it all appears, there are times when it is beyond my imagination."[10]

It is through the eyes of wonder that we will occasionally be able to see the ordinary in just such a remarkable light. Wonder enriches vision by never resting on the surface of a fact or situation. It calls us to push beyond the apparent in order to discover the real. It takes us beyond the familiar to the novel—even in that which is ordinary and commonplace. Wonder transforms perception. It gives us new eyes through which we can see the world and journey deep into its possibilities and nature. In so doing, wonder keeps experience fresh and curiosity alive.

Nothing you do can produce wonder. You can, however, be open to it, and you can welcome it. You can make space for it. As simple a thing as going for a slow, contemplative walk and noticing what catches your attention can open the door to wonder. The setting can be wherever you find yourself. There is no need to go somewhere special. Simply clear the space within yourself and your schedule for a gentle walk in which you make no effort to do anything other than to see with the fresh eyes of attention. Then, after the walk, find a creative way to respond to your experience. You might, for example, write about it in a journal. If you are accustomed to keeping a journal and do so in prose, consider writing a poem. Or you may want to draw or paint a picture, make a soup, or choreograph a dance. Do not view these as works of art. Rather, view them as simply the voice of the soul.

I take contemplative walks like this most days. They are quite different from instrumental walks (to get something or somewhere) or exercise walks because, since the means is the end, I walk slower. I seek simply to open my spirit and soul to the world and to God— to notice and then to allow myself to respond. These are times of prayer—not because I talk to God or think about God but because I watch and listen for fresh soundings of life, for an encounter with that which truly is.

Recently I began to process my experience on some of these walks by writing a poem after returning. The value of this practice does not lie in the quality of the poetry but in the way it supports seeing. Here is a sample from a recent spring morning walk.

> Long shadows in the early morning sun
> Stride like giants
> With coffee cups in hand
> As commuters walk across Selkirk Trestle
> To work.
> Moss—verdant and ripe—releases its moisture
> As, warmed by sun, it joins buds
> And shoots
> And flowering heather and crab apple blossoms
> In reaching out,
> Shaking off winter's grave clothes.
> Everything alive,
> Vibrant,
> Birthed anew,
> Celebrating Life!

What I saw on this morning was not spectacular in any objective sense. However, it was special to me. It was a moment of awareness and enchantment. What I experienced is so small and so subjective that it seems almost trivial. But it is precisely because it can be so easily ignored that it is important to pay attention to it. The gift of wonder begins with the awakening of awareness. Our part is then simply being open to seeing the ordinary in a new light—through childlike eyes of wonder.

The Gifts of Wonder

Wonder has been called the most pregnant human faculty. The richest fruits of human culture all issue from it—art, science, and religion all emerge from the cradle of wonder and curiosity. But it is also full of new life for the individual, not just for civilizations.

Wonder about anything is a pondering that holds the object of our attention gently without having to solve it or figure it out. Mary, the mother of Jesus, is described in the Gospels as pondering in her heart the angelic proclamation that her newborn son was Christ the Lord (Luke 2:11, 19). Wonder is more a matter of heart-pondering than mind-thinking. It is rumination that leaves space for mystery, confusion, fear, uncertainty, awe, paradox, and questions. It receives all of these with soul hospitality and welcome. When we wonder, we stand in awe and wordless stillness. We simply pause and watch to see what may emerge from the fertile soil of our attentive stillness. It is like listening to great music. We receive it in openness without having to try to do anything to it. Rather, we let it do something to us—something that may just be a thing of wonder.

Wonder does, in fact, do things to us. The person who knows wonder is the person whose soul is deepening and whose spirit is expanding. Wonder enlarges us and draws us out of our self-preoccupation. It attunes us to the sacramental majesty of the world. It softens the ego and creates space within us for awe, surprise, and reverence in the face of the mystery of what is. It is, therefore, the natural source of prayer. But prayer that is born out of wonder is not as full of words as prayer that starts with our needs or desires. In fact, it is often wordless. It is this emptiness that allows it to hold mysteries so profound that the only response to them is silence.

This sense of wonder can also help us recognize and appreciate the mystery of our own being. Those who retain a sense of their own mystery possess a vitality that expresses itself in terms of passion to explore and discover new aspects of their life. Wonder leads this exploration inward and downward—into places that analysis can never take us. It opens up space and possibilities. It nurtures the development of gratitude. And it keeps us grounded in the realities of our life and existence that we ponder in our hearts. Wonder invites the wonderful. It awakens awareness to the sacredness of life. It prepares us to witness the transformation of the ordinary into the extraordinary.

Cultivating Wonder

Speaking about the indispensable nature of wonder in seeing God in all of life, Eugene Peterson says the following: "Without wonder we approach life as a self-help project.... Without wonder the motivational energies for living well get dominated by anxiety and guilt."[11] Wonder opens us up to the world and to our life in it. Wonder allows us to see the extraordinary in the ordinary, the sacred in the profane.

There is nothing you can do to generate wonder. However, if it is absent from your life and you have begun to practice awareness, then it may be that you need to make space in your life for wonder. Wonder seldom emerges in a life that is crammed with work, people, words, and noise. Because it always starts with noticing something in a fresh way, wonder requires enough time to allow us to pay attention and enough stillness to allow what we encounter to have its wondrous impact on our souls. If this is your desire, try the following exercises:

- Find a picture of someone you know and love and look at it contemplatively. Don't analyze its details, but open yourself to the picture and the person it represents. Let the impressions that emerge flow over you gently. See if you can discover something about them that you have never seen before or that you have not been aware of as clearly. In other words, look at them with fresh eyes, allowing yourself to see them anew—as if for the first time. Look at their eyes, into their eyes. Dare to stare, perhaps longer than you ever would if they were before you. Allow their eyes to be a doorway through which you can enter the mystery of their being. You may feel like you know them well, but allow yourself to enter their life through this photograph. See if you are able to encounter the stranger that is there in the midst of the familiar and intimate. Be open to the mystery that is, or was, their life.
- Take a walk in a garden or forest. Walk slowly and draw in each breath intentionally and fully, allowing each to fill you up

with the sensations of this place. Continue to do so as you walk around, waiting for one thing—possibly quite a small thing—to command your attention. When it does, turn to that one thing, large or small. It could be a tree, a flower, a petal, or a bug or water drop on a petal. But now focus on that one thing. Take a few moments—longer if you wish—and allow each breath to fill you up with whatever that one thing has to share with you. Notice it. Reflect on it. Ponder it in your senses, imagination, emotions, and thoughts. Again, open yourself to seeing it as if you have never seen anything like it before. And open yourself to its mystery—to the ways in which it is so marvelously exactly what it is—to the elegance, simplicity, and beauty of its being.

✢ If you have never done so before, and particularly if you feel that you have no talent for it, consider taking a few lessons in painting. Notice how you begin to see the world differently as you start to think about how you might represent it on paper. And as you do so, take note of the beauty hidden in the small details. Allow yourself to be surprised by the complexity of colors that previously appeared singular—the enormous variety of shades of green that make up leaves, or the many contrasting colors that combine to form what we think of as the blue of water or the gray of clouds. Look carefully at the richness of texture and notice the way in which you can feel something that you only encounter with your eyes. As your eyes open to these small things, let yourself experience a knowing of the world through eyes of wonder, and observe how different it is from your more usual way of seeing and knowing.

✢ Finally, watch for an opportunity to gaze into a starry sky from a place of darkness. You might do this by means of a visit to a planetarium or astronomical observatory, or you may be able to find a relatively secluded place to look directly and unaided into a clear nighttime sky. If you can, lie on your back and allow yourself to float in wonder among these specks of light that have traveled millions of light-years to get to your retina. Consider that the current estimate of the size of our universe is 156 billion light-years and that it is expanding at that outer boundary at a mind-boggling rate. And consider that cosmologists tell us that ours is likely only one among many universes that lie in the vast space beyond that outer boundary. Allow yourself to experience wonder. You do not have to generate it. But it will be there within you if you are willing to allow its emergence.

Matthew Fox describes awe as the beginning of the spiritual journey.[12] Through eyes of wonder and delight we encounter creation as a mirror of God that reveals God's presence within it. But while we can discern the presence of the divine in sunsets, waterfalls, and rain forests, nowhere is it clearer than in other humans. It is, therefore, to the otherness of others that we turn for the next practice of soulful spirituality.

10

Otherness

In the last chapter we discovered that seeing the world through eyes of wonder enables us to perceive things that would otherwise be missed. Wonder combined with attentiveness enables us to see the extraordinary in the ordinary. This has an important counterpart in interpersonal relations. Here too we need to learn to penetrate the facade of familiarity. Familiarity easily obscures the presence of the unfamiliar stranger in those with whom we are most intimate. Soulful spirituality invites us to do a better job of recognizing and prizing the otherness of others rather than simply seeing them as extensions of ourselves or using them as containers for our own projections.

Honoring the unique individuality of others has deep spiritual significance in that if we fail to recognize the other in people we encounter, we have no chance of discerning the presence of the Transcendent Other. However, if we learn to show hospitality to the stranger that is part of every person we encounter, we are showing hospitality to the Wholly Other who is in them.

I recently met a woman who, on learning that I was writing this book, told me that she did not consider herself spiritual but that her work served her in the way she thought spirituality or religion might serve others. She was a cultural anthropologist who had spent her life studying the Karamojong tribe of Uganda—an ethnic group whose lifestyle has changed little since the eighteenth century. To do this, she lived with them for several years in an effort to understand their experience and see the world through their eyes. It was, she said, a way to fulfill her fundamental passion of deep knowing of others in their uniqueness. This was what made her life worthwhile. It was more basic than her work. It was her life, her deepest value, and the source of her deepest fulfillment. And, I told her, it was her spirituality.

Honoring otherness is a deep and essential part of any authentic spirituality. In its absence there can be nothing transcendent to the self; the self must be its own god. In its absence the holy is so shrunken as to be trivial. If we are to actually encounter the truly holy and the Wholly Other, we must start by honoring the otherness we meet in people. Describing the sacred work of Christian spiritual direction, Margaret Silf suggests that "when we open our heart's experience to each other in trust, we are entering on holy ground where there is no place for comment, criticism, or correction, but only for a response of loving acceptance. On this holy ground God-in-you is listening to God-in-the-other."[1] What she describes is not limited to spiritual direction. It is the truth of any genuine act of hospitality toward the otherness of any human being.

Encountering Otherness

That others are in some important ways not like us is both a threat and a curiosity. Jean-Paul Sartre was most impressed with the first of these two responses, viewing the encounter with the other in decidedly inhospitable terms. The threat lies in the fact that the other has the power to challenge our way of being. Simply by virtue of living from another center of meaning and approaching the world from another vantage point, the other is a threat to the validity of our basic life posture and a challenge to our lived spirituality.

Emmanuel Levinas, who was, like Sartre, a twentieth-century French philosopher, recognized this threat but viewed it quite differently. He described it as a "traumatism of astonishment."[2] In much the same way in which wonder enables us to experience the wondrous all around us, respectful openness to others can provide astonishing benefits to spirit and soul. While the encounter has the potential to be disruptive, it also has the potential to expand our horizons, decenter our ego, and ease the tyranny of our egocentricity. It can also attenuate our self-absorption by challenging us to take seriously an alternate way of being human. Within every encounter with the other is the wondrous possibility of new ways of understanding ourselves and the world and new ways of appropriating truth. The other offers us, therefore, the possibility of fresh and more vital ways of living our life and more authentic ways of living our spirituality.

I didn't actually learn about the spiritual implications of honoring otherness from Sartre or Levinas. The person who first drew this important dimension of spirituality to my attention was my son Sean. He has always been attracted to the otherness of people. It drew him into studies in anthropology and subsequently led to his work in a company that serves people who want to experience the cultures of the world, not simply see the sights. I have always admired the way he meets people where they are and respects their uniqueness. More than that, he is fascinated by what makes them different from himself. I understood when he, as a teenager, told me that he no longer considered himself to be a Christian. I knew he needed the space to find his own way. But when, more recently, he told me that he did not see himself as spiritual—at least not in terms of the picture of spirituality that I had been presenting in my books—I knew that I needed to clarify and broaden the picture. For, as I told him, his eye for the uniqueness of others and his passion to respect this was one of the things that most deeply assured me that his spiritual journey remained well on track.

To say that every human being is an other is to say that each is a person with her or his own unique identity and way of experiencing the world. Ethnicity, education, culture, religion, and class may make us superficially look like each other, but in the depth of our subjectivity and in the contours of our soul, we are absolutely unique. Consequently, no one can ever know another person fully. This is both the great mystery and the great loneliness of our individuality. But, while we can never know another fully, the other person has the capacity to enrich our experience of the world by adding dimensions of his or her otherness. This is the gift that lies beyond the threat of otherness.

Managing the Threat of the Other

We always encounter the other as a face that is both familiar and unfamiliar. It is that unfamiliarity that awakens both our fear and our curiosity. Because the fear is always present as an undercurrent, we often seek to minimize the threat. There are two main ways by which we do this—either by exaggerating the otherness or by minimizing it.

The most common way we deal with the threat presented by a self that is not our self is to exaggerate the difference by treating the other as one of "them" as opposed to one of "us." It is so easy to dismiss and treat as a nonperson anyone we consider to be one of them. Think, for example, of the way we often do not even notice the homeless person we might encounter on the street. Or think of the lengths to which we go to avoid the person with noticeable deformity or disease. Something similar happens in racism, ageism, sexism, weightism, heightism, and other types of ism discrimination. All forms of prejudice allow us to manage the threat of otherness by avoiding encounter with whole classes of people whose differentness makes us uncomfortable. And we do this simply by dismissing them—failing to acknowledge their otherness, sometimes even failing to count them as humans.

The other strategy is to reduce otherness to sameness. This is the preferred strategy with intimates and can be most clearly seen in romantic love. To say that love is blind is, more precisely, to say that love is blind to otherness. Unconsciously we may be attracted by some of the things about the other person that make them different from us, and consciously we may be able to acknowledge the most benign of these. But the fundamental otherness of the other is minimized by treating lovers as basically like us. This may seem like a charitable assumption, but it will inevitably produce problems when the otherness of our intimates can no longer be ignored.

Both these strategies may reduce the threat that would otherwise come with a genuine encounter of the other person in his or her uniqueness. But they also eliminate the opportunities for the enrichment of our lives that this encounter could have brought. Both surround us with the seductively comforting sense of being safely in a place of sameness. This sense of safety is, of course, an illusion because the stranger lives on in the heart of the intimate. Genuine intimacy comes only when that stranger is welcomed and embraced in his or her uniqueness and difference from us. Deep friendship involves befriending not just what the other person has in common with us but the important ways in which she or he is and will always be different from us. It means cherishing the otherness of the other, welcoming and honoring the stranger in the friend or intimate.

Strangers, Monsters, and Gods

If we are honest, though, we have to admit that strangers often still make us uneasy, even after we apply these first-level strategies of managing the threat of the other. There are, however, two additional ways of defusing the danger associated with strangers: strangers can be turned into either monsters or gods.

We manage the first of these transformations by means of projection. This is a variation on the strategy of exaggerating the difference of the other. But in this case, we make the other not only one of "them" (not me and not us) but "it" (against me and us). We effect this vilification by treating the stranger as simply a container for all the parts of our self that we seek to disown. We then dump the despised and feared parts of our self into this container and view the resulting monster as wicked and dangerous. This does not eliminate the fear that was aroused by the stranger. What it does, however, is help us disown the undesirable parts of our self and package them in a way that makes it acceptable to both hate and fear the monster—even to kill it if given the chance.

Turning the threatening other into a god is a bit more challenging, but not as difficult as it might seem. We do it by means of idealization—an unconscious defense mechanism designed to protect us against terror by appeasement. We kneel in vulnerability before this strangely fearsome god, hoping that by acts of contrition and offerings of one sort or another we might avert the danger that the stranger represents. Now fear and awe intermingle, and by virtue of this intermingling, the fear is somewhat diluted.

These two strategies are not as dissimilar as they may seem. In fact, the same type of person is vulnerable to both. In terms of their psychological makeup, these people are associated with what psychoanalyst Melanie Klein called the paranoid-schizoid stage of development,[3] a primitive stage of psychological functioning associated with extremely limited capacity to hold together the good and bad qualities of either self or other. This results in a propensity to both projection and idealization as others are rendered either all bad or all good. Fanatical followers who invest gurus with magical powers and moral excellence at the same time find scapegoats whom they blame for the disasters that often befall these leaders; the scapegoats can be easily sacrificed because they are viewed as evil incarnate.[4]

Tourists and Discoverers

These are not the only ways of responding to the otherness of others. Not all failure to respect and honor the uniqueness of people can be reduced to psychopathology, and things are not always as dramatic as the examples we have been considering. Our openness to other people will be reflected in the types of movies we watch or novels we read, the ways in which we use our leisure time, and the breadth of our circle of friends and acquaintances. Some people spend their whole life within the ghetto of their ethnic or socioeconomic communities, never genuinely getting to know anyone outside of their tribe. Others seem to live in many communities and draw friends and acquaintances from many different worlds.

Our approach to travel will also tell a great deal about our openness to otherness. Think of the difference between two types of international travelers. The tourist—at his worst—visits a new country to collect souvenirs, photos, and another stamp on his passport. He easily complains about the things that are not the same as back home and brushes up against local people and their culture in only the most superficial way. In contrast, the discoverer—at her best—visits that same country to meet local people as a way to enter and know their culture as fully as possible. For her, it is the otherness that is most attractive; for him, it is the sameness. Of course, this is a bit of a caricature. But the differences between these two travelers are remarkably apparent to those who live in the place being visited—likewise, the impact of the trip on the visitors is dramatically dissimilar.

Some live with this sort of openness when traveling, but when at home they settle into a cocoon of safety that insulates them from otherness. We do not have to cross oceans to encounter otherness. All we have to do is be prepared to meet it in the next person who crosses our path. Doing so is the essence of hospitality.

Hospitality

In common usage the concept of hospitality is associated with such things as throwing a great party or entertaining guests. We even have a hospitality industry based on the business of making people feel welcome and at home when they travel. The roots of the concept of hospitality suggest something much richer.

In the West the concept of hospitality comes to us primarily via the ancient Mediterranean world, where it was much more than a matter of entertaining one's neighbors at dinner. According to the commentaries on the Torah, Abraham—the father of Judaism—spent his days sitting at the doorway of his tent waiting to welcome any who passed by. Hospitality began with the provision of food and protection for travelers but also included a bath, supplies for the traveler's onward journey, and an escort along the road toward the next destination. Embodying these ideals of hospitality, Abraham's solicitousness would not have been limited to accommodating the stranger who arrived at the door, but would have extended to running after the ones passing by to press them to accept the gift of welcome that he and his wife, Sarah, wished to extend. This understanding of hospitality became central to Judaism and remains particularly clear in traditional, observant Jewish families as they welcome strangers at Shabbat, the special weekly meal on the Sabbath.

Christians embraced this Jewish tradition of welcoming strangers, as did Muslims. The Christian monastic tradition placed hospitality at the center of its raison d'être. Part of the Rule of Saint Benedict—the founding document that still serves as the operating vision of the Benedictine order—is that all guests who arrive should be received as Christ.[5] It was this that allowed monasteries to serve as the inns of medieval Europe.

Genuine hospitality has enormous potential to enrich relationships. The effects are most spectacular in marriages and other relationships of intimacy, but the principle is equally applicable to all relationships. This is what Jewish philosopher Martin Buber had in mind when he distinguished between "I-Thou" and "I-it" relationships.[6] We relate to someone as a Thou when we welcome their otherness and treat them as sacred. The relationship can then be subject to subject, or personal. In contrast, we treat another as an it—regardless of whether actually animate or inanimate—whenever we engage with them as an object. But to do so, even when done with professional benevolence, is to dehumanize the other by offering them an impersonal relationship. Truly personal relationships demand that we engage the other as a Thou—embracing their otherness and their humanity and in so doing helping both to flourish.

Part of the gift that the other can give us is that he or she has stories to tell us that we have never heard before, stories that may not be easily reconciled with our own stories.[7] These stories will be both enriching and subversive. Dialogue always is. New stories have the power to stimulate our imagining and transform our seeing. They can inspire new ways of living and open up fresh possibilities for understanding our life and the world. They offer, therefore, enrichment for spirit and soul that can never be found when we simply listen to stories that comfortably support our own.

Dialogue

According to Buber, all real living exists in meeting another as a Thou. The place where this happens is in dialogue. In genuine dialogue the other becomes present, not merely in the imagination or feelings, but in the depths of our being. Meeting under these conditions results in each participating in the life of the other. What was between two people is now within each of them. This is the mystery of dialogue.

Dialogue is one of the deepest forms of soul engagement we can experience with another person. Friends share what we generally call conversation. But not all conversation is worthy of being described as dialogue. Conversation can involve little more than passing time through chitchat. At other times it is simply the exchange of information. True dialogue is richer than such simple conversation. Dialogue involves shared inquiry designed to increase the awareness and understanding of all parties. The goal of dialogue is exploration, discovery, and insight. In dialogue I attempt to share how I experience the world and seek to understand how you do so. In this process each participant touches and is touched by others. Inevitably, this results in each person being changed.

Dialogue is rare because it can be threatening and will often be difficult. For many people, the possibility of being changed by the other is simply a deal breaker. For years I have argued for psychotherapy to be practiced as a form of dialogue. However, the prospect of meeting the other person in a place where the therapist, not just the patient, might be changed is simply too threatening for many therapists who view what they do as a technical procedure. Offering psychotherapy in such a way is a clear example of an I-it relationship. Prizing objectivity over subjectivity, the relationship will always be less than fully personal.

Mutuality does not require symmetry of roles. Even in situations where I am recognized as having the primary responsibility for the care of the other person, mutuality can be present if I am able to answer the following three questions affirmatively:

1. Am I willing to bring myself, not just my care, to the encounter?
2. Can I accept the other as a whole and separate person, as he or she is?
3. Am I willing to be open enough to their experience and ideas that my own may change as a result of our interaction?

If I can answer these affirmatively, dialogue can be present. If I cannot, the relationship may involve expertise and empathy, but it will never be an encounter worthy of being called dialogue. Thich Nhat Hanh suggests that in true dialogue, both parties must be willing to change. "We have to appreciate that truth can be received from outside of— not only within—our own group. If we do not believe that, entering into dialogue would be a waste of time."[8]

Many other things beyond the professionalization of relationship and a fear of being changed keep us from such encounters. Some people are so mistrustful of other beliefs and spiritualities and so certain of their own grasp on truth that they are incapable of engaging others deeply except by means of argument or proselytizing. Meeting someone in dialogue always involves at least a temporary suspension of our presuppositions about our selves and the world. This means it also always involves a degree of vulnerability to truth. Others are threatened by the mystery of life in general, which therefore limits their engagement with the mystery of the life of another because doing so might bring them into contact with the mystery of their own life.

A lack or fear of genuine knowledge of one's own self also serves as a major barrier to dialogue. Dialogue is the meeting of two or more selves. What I have to give to others is directly proportional to the depth of my knowledge of my self. If I do not know my self, the only self I have to offer in dialogue will be a false self. But false selves invite and engage with false selves. True and authentic ways of being emerge with difficulty under conditions of an encounter with a false self. But to the extent that I am genuinely and deeply my true self, others who meet me are afforded an opportunity to also be their true selves.

A lack of courage and a fear of intimacy also block genuine dialogue. It takes courage to respond to the invitation to share self with another person. If I am afraid of genuinely meeting another self, I will prefer a conversational form that makes fewer demands on its participants. Genuine dialogue is an intimate encounter. It is not for those who lack the courage to honestly engage with another.

Finally, dialogue is also impaired by a need for control. One can control interviews and conversations, but one must surrender to genuine dialogue. Much like moving into a flowing stream of water, one must enter dialogue ready to let go and be carried along on a journey. We can create opportunities for dialogue and we can participate in it, but we don't actually create dialogue nor can we ever control it. If I must control where I go and where the conversation or relationship goes, I cannot afford dialogue. If, on the other hand, I can temporarily relinquish my need to control myself, others, and my relationship with them, dialogue offers a unique opportunity for an enlargement of the self of all participants.

Ultimate Otherness

Honoring otherness has always been a central aspect of Islam, Judaism, and Christianity, each of which understands that beyond the immanent other is the Transcendent Other. Levinas, speaking as a Jew, makes this point by suggesting that the face of the other always bears the trace of God.[9] We honor the otherness of people because they, like us, bear the image of God—created of dust and divine breath. The other is, therefore, the middle ground between me and God. The possibility of a relationship with another person is grounded in the fact that that person is already in relationship to God. In others, therefore, we encounter the Ultimate Other. And honoring the otherness of other people is honoring the face of the Divine that they reflect.

From a Christian perspective, Richard Norris argues that "goodness for human beings consists in affirmation of the other, and that means both the ultimate other—God—and creaturely others—the neighbor. Human beings are so constituted that their life, growth and fulfillment as persons depends on their openness to the other which addresses them, makes claim on them, and enables them to come out of themselves."[10] This is how important other people are in Christian spirituality. They are often the place of our most direct encounter with God. It is through them that the Ultimate Other often addresses us and invites us to life.

But no one has better understood the importance of otherness to Christian spirituality than Rudolf Otto.[11] It was Otto who first described God as the Wholly Other, arguing that the experience of the holiness or sacredness of God is encountering the otherness of God. If God is the Supreme Other—the one whom we should always encounter with the mixture of fear and fascination that he called *mysterium tremendum*, not simply with casual familiarity that replaces the divine otherness with more comfortable sameness—then our openness to the otherness of those whom Christians believe are created in the image of God will be directly related to our openness to God.

Honoring otherness forms an equally central feature of Jewish spirituality, where the sacredness of the other is also grounded in the sacred otherness of God. The otherness of the Divine is so profound and familiarity recognized to be so dangerous that the divine name is never pronounced by Jews, many of whom write the English word *God* as "G-d" or "Gd."[12] This is the basis for the sacred otherness of humans made in God's image.

The heart of personal life is an encounter with others that we cannot control without destroying. In some mysterious way, each time we honor the otherness of another person and meet them in respect as a Thou, we meet the Divine. Each such encounter holds the possibility of our transformation. Buber described this as the possibility of "healing through meeting,"[13] an idea that Carl Rogers took to the heart of the person-centered approach to psychotherapy that he developed.[14] Healing does not come from what one person does to the other but from what both experience by virtue of the mutuality, presence, vulnerability, and engagement that both offer.

James Mundackal states that "to be is to be related. Everything in the world is being with others."[15] Dialogue helps us glimpse into eternity because it always involves the unpredictable, uncontrollable, and transformational meeting with the otherness that lies beyond my self. This is why prizing otherness and meeting others in dialogue lies right at the core of the life of soulful spirituality. For it is here that we encounter the possibility of relief from the small world of our ego-self. It is here that we encounter that which is truly transcendent to our self. It is here, therefore, that we encounter that around which the self can be integrated and aligned.

Honoring Otherness

To make this more practical, let me end this chapter with several things you can do if you wish to further cultivate your honoring of otherness.

✛ As I suggested in this chapter, one of the places where otherness gets lost most easily is in intimacy. Reflect on the person to whom you are closest. How much of the stranger remains in his or her presence with you? Try to notice and affirm the parts of this person that are different from you—the dreams and passions that are not yours and that may not fit well with yours. Cultivate the safety for both of you to be strong in your own unique persons, and do what you can to encourage the full living out of the parts of this person that you do not understand but that you know to be important threads in his or her sacred otherness.

✛ Do some research on a racial, ethnic, or cultural group about which you know very little—perhaps an indigenous population in your own country or some other part of the world. Try to learn as much as possible about the traditions, beliefs, values, and myths that have shaped these people. Get genuinely curious about their life, not just the facts about them as a group, and follow that curiosity as you seek to really understand what it would be like to experience life as a member of that group.

✛ Do the same sort of research on a spirituality that is quite different from your own and about which you are unfamiliar. It may be one that has long interested you, or one about which you know nothing—not even enough to have whetted your curiosity. If you disidentify with religious spiritualities, consider making one of the religious paths your focus. And if you are religious, consider trying to really get inside one of the nonreligious paths. In either case, approach this learning with empathy and respect, not argumentation. There is no argument to be won or lost. Your goal is simply to enrich your appreciation of the spiritual path by better understanding an expression of it that is quite different from your own.

✛ Now watch for someone in your world who is on a spiritual path that is different from your own and make an opportunity to talk with them about this. Again, don't use this encounter for debate. Consider it rather as an opportunity for dialogue. Listen with empathy and compassion to however much of their story they choose to share. Use it as a doorway into the mystery of their person. Let them know that you appreciate the honor that entering this mystery represents.

When we show welcoming hospitality to the otherness of others, we encounter the gift of a doorway to the broader realities that exist beyond the comfortable place in which we make our home. Embracing these realities—and all reality—is the foundational practice of soulful spirituality to which we now turn.

11

Reality

Three ways of relating to reality are often expressed in terms of a well-known cynical joke that compares neurotics, psychotics, and psychiatrists: neurotics build castles in the air, psychotics move into them, and psychiatrists collect rent from both groups. It is, of course, a bit more complicated than this, but impaired contact with reality is a defining characteristic of psychosis. However, as we shall see, psychotics are far from being the only people who lack an anchor that tethers them securely to the realities of their life.

An embrace of reality always supports the life of both spirit and soul. Both thrive in the soil of acceptance of that which truly is and shrivel when we wander from a commitment to such truthful living. Recall that the journey of the soul is down and into the realities of ordinary life. We damage our soul when we ignore this grounding. If we are sufficiently attentive, we may have some awareness of this inner damage and the crisis that it represents and try to respond to it by spiritual flight. However, any soaring of spirit that occurs apart from a soul anchored in the truths of our lives will be short-lived and unhealthy.

Seduced by Illusion

The truth is that we generally only want truth on our own distorted terms. If we are honest, most of us have to acknowledge our preference for warm, comforting illusions over cold, hard realities. Spinning these illusions is one of the core functions of the defense mechanisms of the ego. Although they accomplish this task in different ways, each illusion distorts the truth of our experience in order to make it more acceptable to us and keep us more comfortable. We all tend to build castles in the air, even those of us who collect rent from our neighbors in the air!

Rationalization is one of the more benign ways in which we distort reality. It involves inventing good excuses to cover real reasons. I may, for example, have a work colleague whom I have never particularly liked and have never forgiven for something I once perceived as a snub. Suppose this person asks me if I am free for lunch. If I think of myself as a friendly person who can get along with most people and who does not harbor resentment or anger, I might turn down the lunch invitation, saying I am too busy. If rationalization is completely successful, I might even convince myself that this is the real reason. But this small distortion of reality simply serves to protect me from the unpleasant awareness that I am not the person I want to believe I am.

A simpler but no less effective version of this is straightforward denial—telling our self (and anyone else who might inquire) that we do not, in fact, feel whatever it is that is unacceptable to us. This is often a remarkably powerful way of distancing our self from unpleasant reality. In the example of the unwanted lunch invitation, denial might even be strong enough to allow me to accept the invitation and eliminate all awareness of my hurt or anger.

As we saw in the last chapter, projection involves a more substantial distortion of the truth of our experience—attributing to others things that we cannot accept in ourselves. By means of projection I might, for example, reinforce my avoidance of my own anger at this colleague by displacing it onto him and treating him as if he is angry at me. If I am capable of this degree of reality shifting—which is the case with many more of us than simply those few who meet the formal criteria of psychosis—I will also likely feel suspicious of his motives for inviting me to lunch. I will probably wonder what treachery he is up to, and my resolve to avoid the encounter will be even firmer.

Reaction formation is an even more dramatic means of denying reality. In this, we display a feeling that is the opposite of what we actually experience, and by so doing, further convince our self that what we wish to avoid is not part of us. Returning to the invitation to lunch, I would be employing reaction formation if I accepted the lunch invitation and said to myself, "I know he is kind of strange and that some people find him a bit rude, but I actually really like him." More remarkable than simply thinking this is the fact that I would both believe and feel it—thus demonstrating the extent of our capacity to live in the castles we build in the air.

By these and many other means, most of us regularly choose illusion over reality. The stories we tell our self become part of a web of lies that binds us. If initially we are aware of what we are doing, it all appears to us to be quite innocent. We might think of it as spin, or possibly positive thinking. However, with repetition it becomes unconscious. The counterfeit reality that we have welcomed into our soul will now grow as it collects around it other illusions and builds itself into a foundation of a life of falsity. It is not so much that we tell lies as that we live them. Worse still, we have become a lie.

The more we live in this place of illusion, the more the harsh light of reality feels threatening. At first our preference is simply to avoid, if possible, facing those things that caused us discomfort. But the longer we choose to do so, the more we need to do so—simply to preserve the self we have built on the web of deception.

The Journey of Descent

Saint Anthony of the Desert, the third-century founder of Christian monasticism, said that the way to ascend to God is to descend into our own reality. When we feel mired down in unwelcome realities, we may be attracted to spirituality because it appears to promise a journey of ascent up and out of these uncomfortable places. However, any attempt to ascend to spiritual mountaintops that is not matched by an ongoing commitment to live in the lowlands of reality will be disastrous. Recall the lesson of the Icarus myth. Be careful of flying too high in your spiritual ambition, particularly if doing so appears to offer the hope of lifting you out of the doldrums of everyday struggles. Spiritual escapism will destroy you. Your wings of wax will melt in the heat of the sun and you will crash. Saint Anthony was right: the journey must first be one of descent into the dark and disconcerting places we seek to avoid.

Without the blood, guts, and gore of day-to-day living in reality, the spiritual journey will always be too otherworldly and disconnected to be health giving. It will become too precious, and our attachment to it will be sentimental and superficial. If God exists and there is a possibility of an encounter, this must be in reality. Thomas Merton suggests that "there is no greater disaster in the spiritual life than to be immersed in unreality, for life is maintained and nourished in us by our vital relation with realities outside and above us. When our life feeds on unreality, it must starve. It must therefore die. . . . The death by which we enter into life is not an escape from reality but a complete gift of ourselves which involves a total commitment to reality."[1]

The path of life will inevitably take us through experiences we would never choose—experiences of depression, failure, illness, suffering, betrayal, abuse, neglect, anger, doubt, confusion, and eventually death. If we seek to avoid the experience of these dark places, we will lose contact with important dimensions of our being. We cannot suppress one emotion without shutting down access to vast regions of our soul. But when we dare to face those demons in the dark places of our interior self, we discover that life can be lived with more intensity, passion, and clarity of vision. We may also find it more genuinely interesting. Life may now begin to provide its own meaning in a way that was never possible when we embraced only the life we thought we wanted rather than the life we actually had. This deeper vision of the mysteries of what it means to be a person may then prepare us for the even greater mysteries that we will encounter if we also follow the journey of spirit.

In the poem "The Guest House," Rumi offers us an important reminder of the gifts hidden in the reality that is our life.

> This being human is a guest house.
> Every morning a new arrival.
>
> A joy, a depression, a meanness,
> some momentary awareness comes
> as an unexpected visitor.
>
> Welcome and entertain them all!
> Even if they are a crowd of sorrows,
> who violently sweep your house
> empty of its furniture,
> still, treat each guest honorably.
> He may be clearing you out
> for some new delight.

The dark thought, the shame, the malice,
meet them at the door laughing,
and invite them in.

Be grateful for whatever comes,
because each has been sent
as a guide from beyond.[2]

Richard Rohr says that God comes to us disguised as our life.[3] But
in order to find God in the realities of our life we must accept those
realities. We cannot be selective in this process, holding only those
parts of experience that we feel ready to accept. We must welcome
all the visitors that come to the guesthouse that is our self. Doing so
will give us depth and substance that we will always lack when we
live in a place of pretense, under the illusion of being in control over
who gets access to our house and who does not. The only choice we
have is whether we receive the guests with welcome or not. To fail to
do so does not drive unwelcome guests away; it merely keeps us from
embracing the reality that is our life.

Living with Authenticity

Authenticity is living the reality that we are. To some extent, we all
confuse this with who we wish to be and how we want others to see
us. We also confuse who we are with what we do (or have done) and
with what we have—allowing our material possessions to serve as
an ego enhancer in the hope that by association we might come to
acquire their attractiveness. There are many routes to the places of
illusion that compromise our ability to live our truth. All damage
the soul because they cut it off from the one thing that is absolutely
vital to its life: truth.

Jesus said that if we live in truth, the truth will set us free. But the
tragedy is that most of the time, we are not even aware that we are not
free. Like the frog slowly dying in water that is being brought gradually to a boil, failing to jump out because it doesn't recognize what
is happening, we are so often oblivious to the fact that our freedom
and life are, little by little, slipping away from us.

Living our truth is coming home to our true self. It is being the only
person I can truly be—my own unique self. The Hasidic tale of Rabbi
Zusia reminds us of both the universal tendency to want to be someone

else and the ultimate importance of becoming one's true self. One day the famous Rabbi Zusia came to his followers. His eyes were red with tears and his face pale with fear. He told them that he had learned the question God would ask him in the coming world about his life. His followers were puzzled. "Zusia," they said, "you are pious, scholarly and humble. What question about your life could be so terrifying that you would be frightened to answer it?" Zusia answered, "I have learned that God will not ask me, 'Why were you not Moses, leading your people out of slavery?' Nor will he ask me, 'Why were you not Joshua, leading your people into the Promised Land?' God will say to me, 'Zusia, there was only one thing that no power of heaven or earth could have prevented you from becoming. Why were you not Zusia?' "[4]

Faithfulness to our true self is being faithful to the most important task of our existence.[5] In all of creation, identity is a challenge only for humans. A flower knows exactly what it is. It is never tempted by false ways of being. Nor does it face complicated decisions in the process of becoming. So it is with cats, rocks, fish, trees, stars, electrons, and all other things. Humans, however, encounter a more challenging existence. We think. We consider options. We decide. We doubt. Simple being is tremendously difficult to achieve, and fully authentic being is extremely rare.

There is, however, a way of being for each of us that is as natural and deeply congruent as the life of the flower. It is a way of being that is unified, not fragmented. Beneath the roles and masks lies the possibility of a self that is unique and authentic. It is not a life that we created. Rather, it is simply living the life that is ours. It is an originality that lies at the foundation of our being and provides an identity that is authentic. Finding and living that unique, authentic self is the challenge on which all our existence, peace, and happiness depends. Nothing is more important.

Over the years I have been seduced by all sorts of substitutes for authenticity. They all came from confusing the self I was with the self I thought I wanted to be. I recall a woman who recently came up to me after a lecture I gave in Manila, telling me she had been a graduate student of mine twenty-five years earlier in Chicago. She said that as she was listening to the lecture, she was struck by how much I had changed. She wished that the soft, gentle person she was encountering now had been her professor, instead of the unreasonably demanding young teacher who was so concerned that everyone would see how much he knew and how little they knew. I recognized the person she was describing. I had thought this was how a young professor ought to be if he was to get ahead and be taken seriously by his students and colleagues. What a joke! But although the joke was on me, it was at the expense of not just me but my students.

Authentic living is grounded in knowing our self. But this knowing is much more than a simple knowing *about* our self as an object. It is a false hope to believe that we can truly know our self simply by learning things about it. The only knowing that opens a door to increased freedom and genuine life is a knowing that is rooted in being rather than thought. It therefore grows out of a response to the invitation to accept our life as it is and to live the gift of life that we have in the midst of present realities. Only here can we live with authenticity.

Because authentic life must be lived in the present, it begins with present realities. Once we stop trying to ignore the aspects of our life that we dislike, our next impulse is usually to try to change them. However, that immediately moves us into a possible future that may or may not ever arrive. Life can only be genuinely lived in the present, and so it is the now that offers the doorway to knowing my self as I am—knowing my self in my being, not my thinking. My life is me. Like a turtle, it is the shell I carry on my back as I creep from one now-moment to the next.

The things I view as crises in my life will usually be the very things that I need in order to draw me out of my fearful hiding from reality. These things have the power to break apart the illusions I have spun around my being and remake me from the foundations. This is the dis-membering and re-membering that is always part of the journey of spirit. Thomas Moore notes that "nothing is more challenging, nothing less sentimental, than the invitation of spirit to become who we are and not who we think we ought to be."[6] However, I must know who I am in truth if I am to become the authentic self I truly am. Any talk about being my true self that does not start with this grounding in reality is simply another expression of a life of illusion.

Listening to Our Life

In his book *Let Your Life Speak*, Parker Palmer argues for the importance of learning to listen to our life rather than simply telling it what we intend to do with it. Our life is not our own in the sense that we can take it and make it whatever we want. The notion that we can become whatever we desire may be part of the American dream, but it is definitely more a part of the dream world than the real world.

Listening to what my life has to say helps me recognize the many parts of my story over which I had no control. The family I was born into, the moment in history I was born, my place in the sibling structure, my family's socioeconomic status, my skin color, my genetic endowment, my body type, my temperament, and even my gender were all beyond my choice. Similarly, although I have had an important role in shaping what my life has become, many factors beyond my control have also been at play in giving me the life that I have.

The writings of Thomas Merton have been a major influence on my life, particularly the things he has had to say about the true and false self and the route to living with authenticity. Something about his voice and life allowed this cloistered monk to reach out beyond his home at the Abbey of Gethsemane in central Kentucky and touch millions of people around the world—people of the Christian faith, other faiths, and no faith. I think that "something" was his own authenticity.

Many people who know him through his books do not know the depth of soul anguish that he had when, late in his life, he fell in love with Margie Smith, a nurse at a hospital in which he was recuperating. He was completely disoriented by the romantic passion that overtook him. Filled with doubts about his ability to continue to follow his vows, he found himself sneaking out of the monastery to rendezvous with the woman who had won his heart. In all of this, however, he was rigorously honest with himself and his spiritual director. His private journals tell the remarkable story of his inner struggle to accept the gifts that this life-disturbing love brought him as he sought to live the existential realities of his life without losing his way.

On June 18, 1966, at the high point of the raging passions that were ripping his life apart, Merton wrote in his journal about the challenges of genuinely embracing these realities and living with the tension they brought. He said that the challenge of life was "to face the real limitations of one's own existence and knowledge and not try to manipulate them or disguise them. Not to embellish them with possibilities."[7] He went on to talk about the enormous danger that lies in confusing the ideal self and the actual self. This, he said, is the life of the false self, something that is particularly tempting for spiritual people who easily convince themselves that they are special and somehow different from and better than others. It might have been humbling to discover the things he heard his life saying to him, but he never turned from this by attempting to deny reality.

Holding the Tensions

Thomas Merton maintained his integrity by honestly accepting the tension that existed between his ideal self and his actual self. He chose to embrace what his life was telling him. This is how we, like Merton, maintain our integrity. However, we must embrace other tensions beyond the gap between our ideal and actual self if we are to live our lives to the full. We must also embrace our inconsistencies.

Even the most thoroughly consistent and apparently integrated person has important crosscurrents of inconsistency in his or her life. The attempt to appear consistent is always a project of the false self. However, rather than making us more integral, this attempt just makes us more unbelievable. The truly alive person always has parts of self that do not fit easily with other parts of self or with expressed values and commitments. We are always a mixed bag of contradictions that will be a mystery to our selves. But these must be embraced if we are to be fully human. As Jesus said in his parable of the wheat and the weeds, "Let them both grow till the harvest" (Matt. 13:30).

Jesus was generally a loving, gentle person—inclusive, gracious, and accepting. But at times he had outbursts of ferocious fury. Think, for example, of his rage at hypocritical religious authorities whom he called blind guides who make others twice as fit for hell as themselves (Matt. 23:15–16). Or think of the day he went to the temple and was so filled with anger over the commercial activities he found within that he took a whip and drove the merchants from the place (John 2:13–17). These words and actions were markedly inconsistent with the "gentle Jesus, meek and mild" of popular perception. They do not represent character flaws, just interesting dimensions of his self that were not generally obvious. The same is true for each of us.

These surprising and seemingly inconsistent parts of character are as essential to fictional characters as they are to us. A thoroughly consistent character might make sense in the context of a soap opera, but in order to be believable, fictional characters must have both enough consistency to be recognizable as a single person and enough inconsistency to be someone with whom we can identify. But perhaps this is not so much a matter of inconsistency as of multiplexity. Our personalities are woven from more than a single thread. Not all are of the same color, consistency, or material. And there is tension when the threads pull against each other.

No one understood this better than Carl Jung, who called the parts of self that do not fit the persona we wish to display our "shadow." The shadow is the dark part of our personality—dark not because it is evil but because it has been judged unsuitable and has been denied access to the light of consciousness and the embrace of the rest of the family of self. It represents repressed parts of self that need to be integrated in order for us to be whole. This integration does not eliminate the tension. Rather, it brings the tension into consciousness, where it can be embraced and managed consciously. Without this step of integration, the tension remains unconscious, and the repressed parts of self are thus much more likely to be expressed by acting out. To deny the existence of inner realities is not to escape their devilish aspects but rather to fall victim to them. To deny inner realities is to fail to truly know one's self, and to not know one's self is to risk becoming possessed by that which we have ignored.

By midlife most of us will be aware of tensions that exist between our limits and potential. We also begin to be aware of what we can expect of our life and what we can no longer reasonably expect. Acceptance of these realities is essential if the illusions of our life are to be shattered and if we are to be able to mourn the life we might have dreamt of but that will never be ours. Without doing this we will never discover the world as it truly is, and our life will always consist of more fiction than biography.

In order to make our life fully real and truly ours we need only to embrace its truths. When we truly accept all that we are, all that we have done, and all that has been our history and experience, then and only then can we be—to adopt the phrase of Florida Scott Maxwell—"fierce with reality."[8] There is no substitute for this fierce engagement with reality when one seeks to live life fully.

Embracing Reality

Properly understood, prayer should be the practice that most firmly anchors Christians in reality. Thomas Merton said that God is far too real to be met anywhere other than in reality.[9] This means that when we attempt to meet God in places of pretense we should not be surprised that God will not be present. Where God will be is in the midst of the realities of our life.

Prayer should be the place where we can honestly share our true self with the true God. This is what gives prayer its transformational potential. Sadly, however, the self that Christians often bring to prayer is our lying, false self—the self we would like to be, or at least would like to be seen by others to be. Often prayer is simply another way that we defend against the truths of our experience. In contrast, prayer that is grounded in reality allows us to meet God in those realities. Prayer then becomes an aid to living with authenticity and being truly alive. For just as God is far too real to be found anywhere other than in reality, so humans are far too real to be able to thrive anywhere other than in reality.

It is never too late to reinforce your commitment to reality. Renouncing illusion is a lifelong process. Consider the following if you wish to live with more authenticity and a fiercer embrace of the realities of your life and existence:

- ✢ What uninvited and unwelcome guests are presently in the guest-house that is your self? Recall that welcoming them does not affect their presence, but it does have a big effect on your spirit and soul. Identify one such guest and see if you are able to make peace with this unwanted part of your experience. Give up your battle with it. You cannot defeat it, so you may as well accept its presence. Do not even bother to label it as good or bad. We are not wise enough to be able to do that, particularly when good gifts can come from guests that we would never willingly invite. Just accept it, and your life, as it is.

- ✢ With what parts of your history and life experiences have you not yet made peace? Making peace with these parts of your story is essential to living in peace with your self and with the world. Consider sitting down with these events and parts of your life at an imaginary table and offering them, one at a time, a declaration of peace. Accept the invitation to be at one with yourself, and in so doing, to be at one with life.

- ✢ If prayer is part of your life, how would it differ if you dared to turn to God in the midst of your present realities—your doubts, struggles, pain, fears, hopes, and fantasies—hiding nothing and holding nothing back? When we speak the truths of our lives in prayer, whatever they are and however we are moved to speak them, we are stripped of the multitude of deceits that infiltrate our being. This is the way in which prayer helps us embrace reality, and this is what mediates its transformational potential.

Embracing reality is a foundational practice of any spirituality that is worthy of being called soulful because reality is the place where spirit and soul meet. Soul calls us down and into those realities, while spirit rises out of them to connect us to the transcendent. But apart from a grounding in reality, both soul and spirit wither, and any spirituality will be nothing but posturing and pretense.

An embrace of reality starts with an embrace of the present moment—being present to myself in that moment allows me to be present to others and to the Ultimate Other. This presence is the next dimension of soulful spirituality to which we turn.

12

Presence

The first time I met Father Basil Pennington, the Trappist monk best known for his work with the form of meditation called Centering Prayer, two things immediately impressed me. Both related to presence.

The first was his physical presence. He was a giant of a man with an enormous white beard, inviting blue eyes, and a warm, playful grin. He was dressed in the black and white Trappist habit with an old black leather belt around his waist, no socks, and black Birkenstock sandals. He looked like Santa Claus in black and white. But it did not take more than a few moments with him for the second thing to strike me—namely, the soul presence that he offered. He was fully with me—attentive to me, available to me, present to me. Nothing from the past or the future seemed to press upon him to distract him. He was simply present in the moment to himself and to me.

Presence and Absence

Humans deeply desire presence. That is why we are so vulnerable to absence and so acutely sensitive to both presence and absence. Absence reminds us of the potential absence of our own being.[1] It confronts us with the basic existential vulnerability that is implicit in birth and explicit in death. Underlying any experience of absence is the echo of the separateness of the self from its Source. Is it any wonder then that we rush to fill experiences of absence with presence of some form or another?

Freud tells the story of a three-year-old boy whom he heard calling out from a dark room in the night. "Auntie," he cried, "talk to me! I'm frightened because it is so dark." His aunt answered him from another room: "What good would that do? You can't see me." "That doesn't matter," replied the child, "when you talk, it gets light."[2] What this child was afraid of was not the dark but the absence of someone he loved. What he needed in order to feel soothed and secure was presence.

In order to be present to ourselves and others, we need others who will be present to us. But we need more than physical presence, even more than polite attentiveness. Think of how often you have been with someone who appeared to be listening but who was instead listening to an inner rehearsal of what they would next say. Or their mind was on some past conversation or future activity. Quite simply, they were not present. What we long for is someone who can be fully with us—present, open, attentive, and available to receive us and our experience. This is not the result of doing or not doing certain things. It is a way of being that is deeply soulful and deeply spiritual.

Stillness, Silence, and Solitude

Being fully present is much harder than it sounds. It is born out of stillness and nurtured by silence and solitude. This triad of guardians of the soul also shapes the formation of attentiveness and wonder, so we need to take a few moments to understand the role they each play in soulful spirituality.

One of the reasons most of us are limited in our ability to be present to others and ourselves is that we possess so little inner stillness. We are too full to be truly still—full of distractions, preoccupations, plans, worries, regrets, things that need to be rehearsed, and things that need to be reviewed. Our inner world is a churning cauldron—endless motion and endless noise. It mirrors our external world. Birds in cities often respond to the incessant urban noise by imitating the sounds of the city, not simply singing their songs of nature. Like birds, we also adapt to our environments. We allow the external noise to mask our inner noise.

Sometimes we say that we long for silence and wish we could be still. We may go to a retreat center or some other place where we can be alone, but when we do we quickly discover that the inner noise and lack of stillness has followed us. Our busyness—which we often blame for our lack of inner stillness—is not the cause of the problem but a way of avoiding it. While we may be attracted to solitude and silence, we also fear them because with each comes an inevitable confrontation with everything we are trying to avoid. External silence confronts us with the realities of our inner world.

Blaise Pascal, a French mathematician and Christian mystic, said that all human evil comes from people's inability to sit still in a room. Peace with myself in stillness is the precondition of being able to be genuinely present to and live peaceably with others. It is me that I want to run from when I am unable to remain at peace in the stillness, silence, and solitude of that room Pascal is watching. The inner demons that surface when I am still, alone, and quiet must ultimately be confronted if I am to be able to be present to myself and others.

Solitude, silence, and stillness each have an inner and an outer dimension. The outer expression of solitude is aloneness. Some times of being alone are essential if we are to cultivate inner solitude, but they are not sufficient. It is inner solitude that is essential—not simply a place where we are alone but a place where we can be present to our self. Inner solitude is a state of peaceful being with my self.

Silence also has an outer and inner expression. One can be externally silent by not talking. While all of us could probably benefit from more of this external silence (those of us who live by our words probably more so than most!), being mute does not translate into inner silence. In fact, we quickly become aware of the difference between inner and outer silence after a day or so of a silent retreat when we may be vocally quiet while the noise from our inner world is deafening. Inner silence is not just refraining from speech. It is being attentive. With inner silence, I move from talking to listening. Most essentially, it is a posture of being open and alert.

Inner stillness is the most difficult of the three, and it is the most important if we are to learn to be fully present in the moment to our self and others. Outer stillness is simply not moving. It is being able to sit in a chair in a room—at least for a while—without getting up and walking around. While this is almost impossible for some, inner stillness—just like inner silence and inner solitude—is challenging for everyone. Inner stillness is letting go. Rather than trying to drive away the distractions, the posture of inner stillness is simply to release them. Being still is, therefore, being free from the distraction of my attachments. It is a state of detachment from all that moves me off center and out of alignment.

Postures of Solitude, Silence, and Stillness

	Outer Posture	Inner Posture
Solitude	Alone	Being present to self
Silence	Mute	Being attentive and open
Stillness	Immobile	Letting go and being centered

Desire and Stillness

We cannot truly become still at our center until we deal with that which pulls us off center. By far the most significant contributors to this decentering are our inordinate attachments and disordered desires.

Taoism has a number of helpful things to say about the cultivation of stillness and the things that destroy it. A Taoist proverb tells us that it is only to the mind that is still that the universe surrenders itself. Stillness is indispensable to the achievement of the four central goals of Taoist spirituality: equanimity, good health, peace of mind, and long life. The anonymous author of the ancient text *T'ai Shang Ch'ing-ching Ching* (*Cultivating Stillness*), argues that the major reason for our lack of stillness is the cravings that come to us from what are called the six thieves—the eyes, ears, nose, tongue, body, and mind.[3] Our mind and senses present to us things that are desirable, and we believe the lie that if only we can possess these things we will be happy. However, the price of our craving is the loss of the stillness that would otherwise be ours. Chasing the illusion that those cravings represent, our mind becomes wild, our spirit distracted, and our bodies out of balance.

Desires are dealt with differently in Christianity, but the practice of detachment is equally important. Jesus taught that love of God and love of money will always be in opposition to each other. "No servant can be the slave of two masters: he will either hate the first and love the second, or treat the first with respect and the second with scorn. You cannot be the slave both of God and of money" (Luke 16:13). But notice that the problem is the *love* of money—not money. When asked which of the commandments was the most important, Jesus replied, "You must love the Lord your God with all your heart, with all your soul, with all your mind and with all your strength" (Mark 12:30). The potential problem with money is the problem with anything that we desire more than God. When we love things more than we love God, we are knocked off center because it represents a misalignment of our being.

Desire is not the enemy of Christian spirituality. It is not, as is the case in Buddhism, the cause of all suffering nor, as is the case in Taoism, the ultimate cause of our lack of stillness. The problem, from a Christian point of view, is not desire, but disordered desire. Desiring anything or anyone more than God robs us of our stillness and makes us present only to our cravings and the illusions they spin.

The Hebrew Bible also contains important teaching on the role of inner stillness. Psalm 46, thought to be possibly written by the prophet Isaiah, presents the following invitation from the mouth of Yahweh: "Be still, and know that I am God" (Ps. 46:10 ASV). The one whose name is "I Am" and whose existence makes possible our own invites us to a knowing that can be found only in stillness. This stillness is letting go of striving. It is being present to our selves and to God. It is a state of being, not simply an achievement of doing or not-doing.

Meditation as Presence

It is easy to make the mistake of assuming that the inner states I have been describing are more readily cultivated by certain people than by others. When talking about contemplative spirituality, people often tell me that meditation simply won't work for them because they are an extrovert. Others tell me that it is obviously a spiritual style that fits women better than men. Neither of these things is true. The truth is that, while we differ in how comfortable we may be with external silence, stillness, or solitude, we will encounter enormous internal resistance when we seek to move these states from behavior to being. This resistance is caused by the things in our inner life that we seek to avoid. This is what follows us to the wilderness or retreat center, and it is the reason that things so quickly return to "normal" once we are back home. The peace that comes from external silence, stillness, and solitude is pleasant, but it is not enough to produce genuine presence to our self or others.

Most spiritual traditions encourage meditation as a valuable resource for the cultivation of stillness of soul. Some people do not like the idea of meditation because they confuse it with prayer and associate it, therefore, with religious spiritualities. Christians sometimes associate it with Eastern religious traditions and assume that it is somehow fundamentally alien to Christian spirituality. However, meditation belongs to neither the East nor the West, neither the religious nor the nonreligious. Most major forms of Eastern religious meditation have corresponding forms of Christian meditation, and those on other spiritual paths can adopt any of these for their own use without abandoning their path or committing themselves to anything inherently religious. The rise of interest in Buddhist meditation in the West is a good illustration of this, as large numbers of Christians, Jews, Muslims, and many others have now made it a regular part of their spiritual practice without in any way identifying with either Buddhism or other religious traditions.

Meditation offers great help in being more present to our self and others. In essence, meditation is practice in presence. It leads us into a place of inner stillness, solitude, and silence, and by doing so, it supports the expansion of awareness. All presence depends on awareness. As John O'Donohue states, "Where there is a depth of awareness, there is a reverence for presence. Where consciousness is dulled, distant, or blind, the presence grows faint and vanishes."[4]

While meditation and prayer share important features, they are not the same—at least as usually practiced. A friend of mine, who for decades has combined Buddhist meditation and Christian prayer, describes the difference by suggesting that while meditation is a technique to focus the mind and help settle into a mode of open receptivity, prayer is more relational in that it involves waiting on, listening to, and allowing one's self to be drawn into God's loving presence. From the outside they may look the same, but from the perspective of the person meditating or praying they will usually be distinct.

Meditative practices fall into three basic approaches. Concentrative methods rely on the focusing of attention. Here the mind is given a simple task (such as counting one's breaths or reciting a simple mantra) so that the deeper waters of one's being can be gathered together in presence. In Islamic spirituality the most common mantra is *La ilaha ill Allahu*—"there is nothing but God"—whereas Christian mantras are often drawn from Scripture. Saint Francis urged his disciples to pray, "My God and my all," repeating this over and over until it emerges as a prayer of the heart and spirit. Father John Main, the developer of a prayer tradition called Christian meditation, recommends a similar use of the word *maranatha* ("come, Lord"). Any short phrase is, however, suitable.

A second group of meditative practices relies on awareness. Here one aligns oneself with an inner observer and simply watches the flow of energy as thoughts and emotions ebb and flood. This is central to most Buddhist meditation. Doing this, one learns to disidentify with the contents of consciousness (thoughts and emotions) and sink into deeper awareness of spiritual realities.

A final group of meditative approaches is based on surrender. Here there is no need to watch thoughts or emotions. As they—or anything else—emerge into consciousness, you simply let them go. Whatever you become aware of you gently release. The goal is not to empty yourself or to make yourself still but simply to be totally open. The best example of this approach to meditation is Centering Prayer. Because surrender is so central to the Christian approach to the spiritual journey, Centering Prayer is deeply congruent with Christian theology and spirituality.[5]

Meditation can take many forms, but its primary goal is always to help one heighten spiritual awareness through increased presence. It is, therefore, an important discipline of soulful spirituality.

Letting Go

In Jill Price's recent autobiography, she describes herself as the woman who can't forget, and the neuroscientists who have been studying her mnemonic abilities agree that this appears to be literally quite true.[6] She has the uncanny ability to recall almost everything she has ever seen or experienced since age fourteen. But this continuous, automatic, autobiographical recall is a mixed blessing. What her story makes clear is how important letting go is if we are to move on in life.

Letting go is an important spiritual practice, but it is counterintuitive because the default posture for most of us is to clutch, not to release. If we are to be truly present to our selves, we must let go of the preoccupations that fill us up and keep us from stillness and presence. To be fully present means that I must be temporarily absent to the things I normally carry with me in consciousness. They are the noises that drown out inner silence, the distractions that keep me from a deep presence to my self and my world. For when I am caught in the rut of my ordinary inner self-chatter, all I am present to is this background static.

The person who is capable of giving this gift of presence is a person who has learned to let go of not just preoccupations but also their self-importance. Often we are too full of ourselves to be genuinely available for others. Some people I know hang on so tightly to the persona they have cultivated as their presence that they may well be present—sometimes in a larger-than-life fashion—but their presence leaves little genuine room for another person's. I recall a powerful businessman I once worked with in psychotherapy. It didn't take more than thirty seconds with him to see why he was so successful. He was intelligent, confident, articulate, interpersonally smooth, and accustomed to being in charge. But it also didn't take long to understand why he had chewed up and spit out three wives and many more senior managers and associates. The presence that he had cultivated as a way to obtain and maintain power left no space for anyone else. There wasn't enough emptiness to allow him to be genuinely present to anyone else.

Genuine soul presence to others always starts with making soul space for them. That space must first be cleared and prepared, which requires setting aside things that normally fill that place. Emptying must precede any genuine presence. Fullness leaves no room in the inn of our soul for guests. Paradoxically, fullness of living and becoming requires emptiness and spaciousness in our being.

The Soul's Aura

Like the businessman I referred to above, however, we all have some sort of presence. It is the way others encounter our individuality. It is alive and dynamic, often entering the room before us. It is the leading edge with which we move through life. We might think of it as the soul's aura. Most of us intuitively know how to read this sphere of interpersonal presence. We know when we are with someone who is angry, fearful, manipulative, or behaving seductively, just as we know when we are with someone who is deeply loving, peaceful, or content. We may make mistakes in our reading of this presence, but that does not mean that it is not real. It is the whole atmosphere that moves with the person.

Animals are often highly attuned to the presence of humans. Notice the way a cat will approach one person (often the one who dislikes cats) while ignoring another (strangely, often the one who is crazy about cats). Just as they can often sense physical atmospheric changes associated with impending storms, animals are quite adept at reading humans. What they are reading is the person's presence.

Presence always influences us, whether we are aware of this fact or not. Although some people's presence may be confused and hard to read—often because of their self-absorption—seldom is it neutral. We may or may not be conscious of a person's soul influence on us, but usually their presence will make us want to either draw closer or move away. Presence will register on our souls even when we are unaware of it. Most of us read presence more in our bodies than in our minds. Our bodies are the screen onto which presence is projected. Here we either experience resonance or dissonance, safety or danger, attraction or fear—or any of the other bodily reactions that we may have but that will often remain outside of awareness.

Knowing something about our own presence is essential if we wish to be present to others in a way that invites them to be present to themselves. I have long known that I have more power in most relationships and situations than I want. I recall a good friend in high school telling me that I was ambivalent about leadership. What I was ambivalent about was my capacity for influence. I knew it was large but wasn't sure what sort of influence I wanted to have. As I became clearer about what I wanted to do with my personal power and how I could use it in ways that were congruent with my sense of calling, my presence carried less and less of that ambivalence. Better understanding my natural presence allowed me to better offer the soul hospitality that I wanted to offer.

Practicing Soulful Presence

Soulful presence is like a still pond. It offers a nurturing, reflective space to all who gather by it. As we are received in hospitable presence, we are given an opportunity to see our own image in the stillness that lies at the center of our soul host. Consequently, we are able to live our own life more fiercely and passionately because of the still, quiet place of presence that we were given. This is a gift of immense value. It is a gift that we can only give others when we have learned to first give it to ourselves.

Presence is a gift, but it is also a practice. It is something we can do that will enrich our inner life and allow us, simply by our being, to do the same for others. Consider the following if you wish to make such soulful presence more a part of your life:

- ✠ Multitasking is an enemy of presence, as is efficiency. Give yourself permission to be inefficient. Practice doing only one thing at a time for periods of time each day. When you are eating, for example, give that your full attention. Notice the taste and texture of each thing you put into your mouth. Treat it like a tasting, not a refueling. Or, if you are looking at something, really look at it. Be present to it. Notice everything about it that you can. Slow down and savor each moment of your life. Really live it. Do not let it simply pass through you without awareness. Be present to it, and to yourself in it. Witness everything that happens in and around you. In so doing, open yourself to the wonder of your life and your world.

- ✠ The next time you are with someone to whom you desire to be more fully present, notice and name the things that distract you from presence to this person. As each is named, allow yourself to release it. If it was something important for you to think about, you will have later chances to do so. Because you have named it you will be quite able to get back to it if you choose. Simply naming it and releasing it is a way that you can quickly increase your presence to the moment and to the other person.

- ✠ Find a time and place where you can be quiet and alone for at least twenty minutes. Gather yourself together in stillness. Now select a word or short phrase that represents for you the Source of All Goodness. This may be a name for God (e.g., Lord, Spirit, Jesus, or something similar) or a word like *love*, *life*, or *trust*. Say this word to yourself each time you become aware of anything, allowing the word to release that awareness. Do not try to stop thinking or to think about anything in particular. Simply release whatever you notice that you have attached yourself to—thoughts, memories, feelings, or anything else that drifts into awareness. Don't say the word over and over; just repeat it whenever you become aware of anything. Then gently return to a place of openness, stillness, and presence. This is the practice of Centering Prayer.[7] Consider making it a daily practice during a time of stillness and presence to your self, to life, and to God.

Without presence we will never know Ultimate Presence. Richard Rohr points out that Jesus's invitation to Martha in Luke 10:38–42 was an invitation to presence—the one thing she was not offering as she scurried around trying to be a good hostess to Jesus when he visited in her home. He suggests that to be present is to keep "your heart open, your mind without division or resistance, and your body not somewhere else."[8] Presence, in a word, is openness—openness to the present moment and to an encounter with our selves, others, and God. As we will see in the next chapter, this openness involves letting go of things that block our presence, a dimension of soulful spirituality that I call surrender.

13

Surrender

Most of the things we have discussed to this point (increasing awareness, cultivating wonder, honoring the uniqueness of others, being grounded in reality, and learning to be fully present) would generally be viewed as good things by most people—even those not interested in spirituality. This is not, however, the case with surrender. Instinctively we do not want to surrender. It feels like something a person should only do when they have absolutely no other option. Fugitives surrender when there is no possible escape. Armies surrender when they face imminent and certain defeat. Surrender under any other circumstances seems to be a mistake that compromises one's autonomy and potentially places one's self in great peril.

This is undoubtedly a very reasonable way to think about it if surrender is understood as submission to power. However, submission to power has nothing whatsoever to do with the sort of surrender that is central to either the spiritual journey or the human developmental journey.

Both men and women tend to have a natural aversion to surrender. For men, surrender usually feels like failure or defeat. The male ego thrives on success and, consequently, most men resist accepting defeat at all costs. Surrender also feels like a threat to men's autonomy.

Sometimes the anxiety associated with such a threat is extremely high, as if surrender would result in the annihilation of their very self.

To women, surrender often feels dangerous because of its association with abuse and the use of power to subjugate. It suggests passive yielding to something that should be actively resisted. It implies power-lessness that could leave them vulnerable to exploitation and mistreatment. Submission in the face of malevolent power obviously carries great potential peril. Clearly, it is important to be very careful about who or what we surrender to, as it can lead to abuse, even death.

And yet, properly understood, surrender is an indispensable gateway to life, genuine freedom, and deep humanity. It will always be misunderstood when it is viewed from the perspective of the ego—our usual vantage point on life—because, to the ego, surrender is diminishment. This is precisely why it is so important. As we saw earlier, ego is essential for human functioning, but when it is not aligned with anything greater than or beyond itself the egocentricity that results will limit the freedom of our spirit. From the perspective of the ego, surrender is the squeal of the pig on its way to slaughter. But from another perspective, we can think of it as a birth scream—the first gasp of breath after a rebirth as surrender ushers us into a new movement of life and a new stage on the journey.

The Illusion of Control

Autonomy and control are cardinal virtues in the West. As young children, we are praised for being big boys or girls when we learn to control our bladders, walk on our own, or put on our own socks and shoes. Control is rewarded and lack of control punished. Soon enough we begin to get the point. We learn that if we are to receive the love and esteem of others it is essential that we be in control—or at least appear to be. Control becomes synonymous with responsibility. To be a responsible adult is to take responsibility for one's self, which includes taking control of one's life.

The ego understands this very well. Control is its modus operandi. The ego knows that control is essential for success and mastery, and so it sets this as its primary task—control of our drives and impulses, control of emotions, control of our behavior, and control (as much as we can) of how others see us. This is why we speak of the ego as the CEO in the organization of the self.

Life brings many opportunities for ego to learn surrender. The first confrontation with external realities over which we have no control is birth. No fetus feels ready for being thrust into a world that at first will be experienced as unimaginably harsh. The first few years of life will inevitably bring many more opportunities to learn that we are subject to forces beyond our control, and the developing ego will take many hard knocks in this process. Like the little train that keeps saying to itself, "I think I can, I think I can," slowly we are seduced by the illusion that we can, if we try hard enough, control our life. We pretend to be in control, and even if at some level we know this is not actually true, we remain committed to acting as if it is. It feels like the natural way to be in the world. But it is a way of being that cuts us off from life.

At times, however, we are all forced to acknowledge our very limited real control over what happens to us. We become seriously ill, we experience the death of someone or something dear to us, and we encounter reversals in life that take away that which we have so assiduously collected and clutched. We may feel powerless and insecure. We may even feel fearful about the future or anxious about the present. These are thin places, pregnant with spiritual possibilities. They represent transitional moments on the journey. Old familiar ways of being are falling apart, and our instinct is to grasp at their remnants and try to patch them back together as a way to restore our sense of security.

Our first reaction to the unwelcome presence of events over which we have no control is usually to brace ourselves against them. We resist things that we cannot run from but that we desperately want to avoid. We may also feel anger at these reminders of our powerlessness. They seem like a violation of some implicit contract—a betrayal of our right to be in control of our own life. We resent the disruption to our life plan that they represent because they challenge the illusion that we are in control.

But while these times feel like they are full of great danger, they are, in fact, full of great promise. These are the moments when it may just be possible to change our fundamental orientation to life. They are invitations to surrender the dominance of our ego and its relentless demands for control. Leaning into them may be frightening, but failing to do so will always mean the loss of an opportunity for growth. We may have future chances, but resistance reinforces resistance, and so each one offers a progressively smaller and smaller window of opportunity.

The Religious Core of Addiction

The reason surrender forms such an important part of 12-step spiritualities such as Alcoholics Anonymous is that control is a foundational dynamic of addictions. Our real addiction is not to things like alcohol, drugs, or pornography but to control. We desperately try to control our feelings, our impulses, our selves. We use substances and ritualized behaviors as ways of distracting ourselves from what we seek to avoid—our failure, shame, and brokenness. The things to which we seem to be addicted are the masks behind which we hide our real addiction. What we are most deeply addicted to is the illusion of control. We are all addicts. We are all addicted to playing god. This is the religious core of addiction—any addiction.

Being human involves enormous vulnerability and risk. Often, therefore, we choose the bondage of addiction over the anxiety and freedom that comes with living life fully alive, fully awake, and fully aware. The primary function of any addiction is to numb and desensitize. Task number one is to keep us asleep and unaware. Regardless of whether our addictive behaviors revolve around food, excessive work or exercise, or sex, the goal is to anesthetize us to the terrors of real living in the face of the unavoidable mystery of being human. It is this terror that we most want to control and from which we most want to escape. The demon in the dark of our inner basement is nothing more or less than our fear of being fully alive.

This fear makes it hard for us to accept our finitude. The illusion of control and the possibility of managing life as opposed to living it keep us forever trying to get it right or, if we cannot do this, at least to fix things that go wrong. It keeps us saying "I can" when the truth would be to acknowledge "I can't." It keeps us pretending that we are god rather than putting our trust in something or someone greater than our ego-self.

Addictions have one more important function. Not only do they distract us from such things as the existential terror of living and our agenda of control, but they also mask a most surprising longing—a longing to surrender. This deep desire is, of course, opposed by an often equally strong wish to avoid surrender. But deep within us we are aware that ego is a usurper. Somehow we know that we are neither the center of the universe nor should ego be the center of our being. At some deep level of spirit we know that we were meant to live in alignment with forces transcendent to our self. We long to be able to face the uncertainty and uncontrollability of life with confidence and with a sense of safety that can never be delivered by the inflated ego pretending to be god. We long to be able to put our trust in someone or something greater than us. The truth is that we must all surrender to something or someone. To refuse to find our place in relation to that which transcends the ego is to surrender to addiction and to the illusion of being in control. If we do not become free in relation to the something or someone larger than our self, we become unfree in relation to tyrannizing powers within our self that we have inflated to godlike proportions.

Inner Nonresistance

Dag Hammarskjöld, the Swedish diplomat and former UN Secretary-General, once said, "I don't know who, or what, put the question, I don't know when it was put. I don't even remember answering. But at some moment I did answer 'Yes' to someone or something. And from that hour I was certain that existence is meaningful and that, therefore, my life, in self-surrender, had a goal."[1]

Saying yes to life—whatever it brings—is a posture of nonresistance to life. It is quite different from resignation. Resignation is an outer posture; surrender is an inner one. Resignation is giving up; surrender is accepting. But it is important to note that what you accept when you surrender is not the total situation but simply present realities. You might still work to change the overall situation. For example, if the bank has foreclosed on your mortgage and you have lost your home, it is quite possible to accept the reality of this loss and yet still seek to restore financial security and suitable housing. You may be unable to keep your home or the life you have built, but you can accept with a total absence of inner resistance a reality that you have not, nor would ever have, chosen. Surrender is simply inner acceptance of what is. There is probably nothing more difficult for humans. But there is also nothing more freeing.

Saying yes to life leads to a dramatically different spirituality than saying no. Each builds momentum for more of the same. A life of resistance leads to willful determination, resolute defiance, and an inner self that grows harder and more brittle. It also leads to a sense of separateness from life—the gap between inner and outer reality increases as the external world is viewed as the enemy, something to be dominated and controlled. In contrast, a life of surrender leads to willingness, openness, and an inner fluidity and flexibility that allows spirit to soar and soul to send roots deep down into a grounded life. Life is the river in which we flow, and in surrender we simply acknowledge that we are capable neither of making it move nor of blocking or reversing its flow. We have only two choices—to go with the flow or to resist it. Resisting the flow does not change our circumstances; it only changes us. And those changes are generally bad.

Surrender invites us to a radical but always freeing posture of nonresistance to reality. It heals our relationship with life and begins to allow life to flow through rather than around or over us. It unifies our interior and outer worlds and allows us to discover new levels of openness to and intimacy with others.

Daring to Welcome Life

I am always astounded when I meet people who have suffered deeply and yet tell me that even if they were able to do so they would never exchange their former life for their present one. I think of a woman I met at a recent conference on spirituality and suffering who told me of her long journey with trigeminal neuralgia—a searing electric shock–like pain that comes from any stimulation, even the slightest air current touching a trigger area on one's face. She told me that she was constantly aware that the next incident could come any time and would instantly envelop her in pain. But she also told me of the way her suffering had opened her to life and deepened her engagement with others and God. Almost unbelievably, she said that she had come to view the disorder as a gift—a gift that she would never have chosen but for which she was now deeply thankful.

I also think of a man I recently met whose wife had died in a tragic car accident two years earlier. They had been very happily married for twenty-six years. He told me of the depth of his grief and the profound sense of the tearing of the fabric of his life that her death had brought. He told me that about a year after the accident he became aware that he had been responding as if he too had died in that accident. Although he was still physically alive, he realized that in his retreat from life he had been embracing a slow death. Gradually he began to sense an invitation to release his former life in order to be open to new possibilities for life that lay ahead. Turning this corner without any idea of what specifically he was choosing, he began to find himself changing in ways he could not have anticipated. He noticed that he began to soften and become more open and trusting. Friends who had known him for years told him he seemed like a different person—gentler, more loving, less driven and intense. He agreed, saying that he had changed so much in his way of relating to life that if his wife could suddenly come back they would need to start all over again to find a way of relating. It was as if he had indeed become a new person, wonderfully healthier and more whole. As great as his old life had been and as much as he continued to miss his wife, he said that even if he could, he would not reverse the events of the previous two years.

I also think of a friend in New Zealand who, as I write this, is dying of cancer. After several long periods of remission, it is clear that the end is near; cancer has suddenly appeared throughout her body. She has been told that she likely has no more than two months to live. At fifty-three years of age, she has everything to live for—a loving family, devoted friends, richly rewarding work, a new music CD that is on the verge of being recorded, a book that will not likely be finished now, and as many dreams as any of us could ever have. However, in spite of this, she tells me that in some strange way that she cannot explain, she knows that the timing of her death is good and that she is fully at peace with it. This is not the voice of depression or despair. It is the voice of a woman who has already begun to experience the good gifts that come from letting go. Even though she is in the valley of the shadow of death, she is bursting with life. Let me share her words directly.

Every connection I make with someone these days is precious and rich. I feel satiated with love and grace. In a way I cannot explain, although my remaining time is short, I believe I am entering the most fruitful time of my life. I am experiencing the truth of that as I meet with people in totally uncensored warmth and dialogue. Life has never been so rich, and I reckon there's only so much of this level of beauty the human heart can take before it explodes! I am firmly at peace and not afraid. I feel surrounded by God and satisfied that I have lived my life well and invested it fully in the people entrusted into my care. A life well spent and thoroughly lived is a peace-producing thought.[2]

Blessings and Misfortunes

How can good gifts be a part of great loss, or blessing emerge from pain and suffering? Conventionally, of course, we are taught to view things like pain as bad and freedom from pain as good. But the experience of those who have learned to welcome what comes to them in life reveals that, when it comes to life experiences, the labels of "good" and "bad" are completely illusory and often seriously wrong. At best, they reflect a limited perspective. Only with the passage of time can we begin to separate out the blessings and misfortunes contained in any development in life. When we are able to do this we will often notice that the greatest blessings lay right in the midst of the things we would instinctively think of as our greatest calamities.

The story of the wise camel driver illustrates this truth. One day a poor man who lived by guiding camels across the desert found a bag of gold coins at an oasis. His friends were happy for him and told him how lucky he was. In reply, he smiled and said, "Maybe." Not knowing what to do with the coins and having nowhere safe to leave them, he carried them with him as he continued to travel. However, word of his luck spread quickly, and a short time later a band of brigands tracked him down, robbed him of his newfound wealth, and left him and one companion to die in the desert with no food or water. His companion cursed him and said what a fool he had been to travel with such an unlucky man. The camel driver again merely smiled and said, "Maybe I'm unlucky, and maybe not." But again, his fortunes soon changed as a passing caravan came by and he was taken back to the village where his family lived. "How lucky that you were not here yesterday," the villagers said on his arrival, telling him how fire had started and quickly destroyed much of the community. Once again, he simply smiled and said, "Maybe." He was a wise man because, instead of trying to evaluate the experiences that were part of his life, he simply chose to accept them without resistance or judgment.

Although we often think otherwise, we are not in a position to judge what is. We can either resist or yield, but we cannot change what is. When we resist we become bitter and resentful. Life becomes the enemy, and our attempts to control it become more obsessive. The shell of our ego hardens, and we become more closed and rigid. To accept what life brings to us is to enter into alignment with reality, which, as we have seen, is a fundamental feature of soulful spirituality. Surrender opens up new dimensions of self. If action is either possible or necessary, that action will now emerge out of inner stillness and presence and not simply be emotional reactivity or behavioral impulsivity.

Welcoming Prayer

Welcoming life does not mean that we will not have preferences about what it might involve. Most people will always prefer pleasure to pain. However, you do not have to choose things to welcome them. In fact, welcome is most applicable precisely in relation to those things that we would never choose and that enter our life as unwanted.

But it is not just life circumstances that we either resist or welcome. The same is also true of our emotional responses to life experiences. Think, for example, of suddenly being cut off in traffic by a danger-ous driver who swerves in front of you, honking his horn and making rude gestures as he passes. For most of us, our instant response will be anger. We may not want to be angry, but the choice is not whether to have or not have that immediate emotional reaction. The choice is how to respond to it once it arrives on the scene. The practice known as Welcoming Prayer provides a framework for how to respond to emotional upset with a spirit of surrender. It involves a three-step process: focus, welcome, and letting go.[3]

Before we can welcome an emotion, we must first focus on it and thus bring it into the center of consciousness. We must face it directly and feel it as a sensation in our bodies. If you are angry, the first step is simply to be present to that anger. Notice where in your body you are holding the energy of that anger. If you are driving your car, per-haps you are now gripping the steering wheel with white-knuckled ferocity. Or maybe your jaw is clenched or your stomach in a knot. Keep your focus on that place, wherever it is. Do not judge, analyze, or try to control the feelings or sensations. In fact, do not even try to change them. Just focus on the sensations in your body and be pres-ent to them. Doing so is much harder than it sounds, but it is the key to the entire process of surrender. We can only release things that we have first acknowledged.

The next step—welcome—seems strange when the emotion is natu-rally unwelcome. Our natural response to fear, anger, depression, anxiety, or other unpleasant emotions is to do whatever we can to push them out of our awareness. Because these emotions are unpleasant, we try to distract ourselves from them. We treat them like the enemy. Something quite remarkable happens when, instead of following this well-worn path, we welcome these unpleasant emotions as a guest in the home of our self. When resistance is replaced by welcome, we remove the power of these unchosen events to disturb our peace. Once we respond to them with hospitality, their disruptiveness to body, spirit, and soul begins to diminish—sometimes with astounding speed. The simple act of gently saying, "Welcome, anger" (or whatever disruptive emotion has suddenly arrived on the scene) expresses a soul hospitality that grounds you in the present and in your body and refuses to allow the external experience to chase you out of presence.

It is important to recognize that what you welcome is your inner response to the present moment, not the whole set of circumstances that might surround it. For example, if you have just been robbed, you are not welcoming the violation and assault, just the anger or other emotional reaction. Similarly, if you have just been given a diagnosis of cancer, it is not the cancer that you welcome but the fear or anger that might accompany this news. The surrender that is being encouraged through this practice of Welcoming Prayer is an inner release, not an outer practice. It is a response of spirit that brings life to body and soul.

Letting go—the core of surrender—is the final step in this process of Welcoming Prayer. What we must release is not simply the negative feelings but also the assumptions that lie behind them. As human beings, we seem to believe that we need three things in order to be happy: control, approval, and security. But this is a lie. We don't need these things to be happy. In fact, pursuing them is the primary cause of our unhappiness and lack of inner peace. What we need to release, therefore, is our attachment to the assumption that we need these things. We need to release our desire for control, approval, and security, and we need to release our desire to change the circumstances of our lives over which we have no real control. These are the things that lead to our unhappiness.

The Spirituality of Letting Go

All spiritual paths can be reduced to two: the way of ascent and the way of descent. The spirituality of ascent seeks ego actualization and focuses on acquiring and mastering competencies that will allow one to live more successfully and with more fulfillment. The spirituality of descent seeks ego diminution and relativization and finds this in surrender. The path of ascent involves shoring up the ego, while the path of descent allows the overinflated ego to spill some of its hot air of self-importance. Donald Trump illustrates the spirituality of ascent when he says, "Show me someone with no ego and I'll show you a big loser."[4] Referring to Jesus, John the Baptizer illustrates the spirituality of descent when he says, "He must grow greater, I must grow smaller" (John 3:30).

The way of ascent is the way of control, willfulness, grasping, and clutching. The way of descent is the way of surrender, willingness, and letting go. Nothing that we fail to give away will ever really be ours. Only that which has died can be raised from the dead.

Surrender alone provides relief to the overinflated ego and, once it gives up playing god, allows it to return to the tasks it can actually accomplish. The ego will never surrender easily. Yet surrender is its only hope. For it is in surrender that the ego can align itself with forces beyond itself and the whole person can find his or her place of belonging in life.

Surrender is integral to Christian spirituality because, properly understood, Christian spirituality is a path of descent, not ascent. Rather than being a spirituality of self-improvement and movement up a ladder of successive approximations to holiness, it is a spirituality of following Jesus on a journey of dying to our false self so that we might discover our true and larger identity in Christ. Self-emptying is the core reality underlying every moment of Jesus's human journey. Cynthia Bourgeault describes Jesus's journey as follows: "Self-emptying is what first brings him into human form, and self-emptying is what leads him out—returning him to the realm of dominion and glory. Whether he is moving up or down the great chain of being, the gesture remains the same."[5]

But Christians are not the only ones for whom surrender is the route to life. As Jesus paradoxically pointed out, life lies on the other side of death. In order to truly find our life we must first lose it (Matt. 16:24–25). And so in surrender we give up that which we think we already have, only to discover that for which we most deeply long.

Choosing Surrender

Life brings us a steady flow of opportunities to practice choosing surrender. Events that we would never choose enter our life quite regularly—sometimes as small interruptions to our plans for the day, and other times as crises that change our life forever. Regardless of their magnitude, these events serve as reminders that, despite our efforts and desires, we are not in control. Despite what we might wish, we are not masters of our fate. We do not choose the time or circumstances of our birth, and most of us do not choose the time or circumstances of our death. Our only choices are what we do with the time we have and how we respond to the things that become part of our story during that time.

Only when we are willing to recognize that we do not control life can we truly say yes to it. Only when we welcome the unwanted can we be free of our natural upsetting reactions to it. These reactions cage our spirits, darken our souls, and damage our bodies.

Consider the following suggestions if you wish to practice the choice of surrender:

- ❖ Watch for the next small, unchosen, and instinctively unwelcome event that enters your life. Notice your initial response to this event. Notice the emotions that quickly arise, and notice the way you experience these in your body. Don't try to change anything. Just stay with those feelings and body reactions until they are clearly in your focus. Name them. And then welcome them. Speak this welcome, even if you do not feel the hospitality that the words imply. Imagine yourself as the host at the door of your self and accept these visitors into your self. Then gently release them.

- ❖ Surrender also has a very important role to play in the resolution of loss. Identify something that you have lost in recent years and that you still miss. It may be a friend, a job, your health, your sense of hopefulness and optimism, your sense of virility and personal power, your feeling of being young, your beauty, the esteem of someone important to you, your own self-respect, or any number of other things. While there is nothing you can do to turn back the clock and recover what is no longer yours, you can release it. Letting go of something that is gone does not mean that you would not welcome it back. It simply means that you choose to let go of your attachment to it. Surrendering that which has been lost is saying, "I acknowledge that I do not need this for my happiness and fulfillment. I thought I did, but I was wrong. I release my attachment to it and move back to a full embrace of life."

Surrender may be counterintuitive—and certainly is countercultural—but it is an essential part of the path to fullness of life. It is the posture of openness that allows life to flow through us rather than us attempting to control life. It is the capstone of soulful living and the place where soulfulness most directly meets and is informed by Christian spirituality. It is essential if we are to become deeply alive and fully human.

Epilogue

Being at One

The journey of becoming fully human is a journey of becoming all we can be. Soulful spirituality is a unique resource in this pursuit. Grounding the spiritual journey in the human journey, as these foundational spiritual practices do, ensures that we are part of this great transformational quest.

Life is a restless movement of becoming. Like water trickling down the side of a mountain, life will eventually find its course. That path will lead it by stagnant pools, through rapids, over falls, and up against seemingly insurmountable obstacles. But life will make its way as it evolves from trickle to stream to river and eventually to lake or sea.

Becoming all we can be as humans is participation in this grand evolutionary adventure. By offering our consent to the pull of Spirit-in-action, each of us co-operates with this great drama of human becoming by being attentive to our own personal journey of being and becoming. At the core of this journey is the transformation of our identity. The foundation of our identity is that with which we identify—whether this is our body, our self, our family, our community, our nation, our religious tradition, our fellow humans, or all living creatures. This journey from egocentricity through ethnocentricity to "lifecentricity" is a journey of broadening perspective based on expanding identifications. It is a journey of releasing the exclusiveness of good identifications for better and bigger ones. It is consenting to the wooing of the Spirit calling us toward fullness of being and actualization of our human personhood.

But notice how this journey also moves us from isolation to deeper communion and, eventually, to union. The single drop of water that starts on the mountainside is joined by others and ultimately finds its place in the river and then the sea. As we journey from egocentricity to Self, we escape the prison of our isolated individuality and discover ourselves to be in the ocean we were seeking to find. We don't create this larger self, nor is its realization our achievement, but we do have to be open to the gifts and invitations of life that call us to our true home, our true self, our self-in-God.

This is a journey from fragmentation to integration, from alienation to alignment, from part to whole. It is a journey toward being at one—at one within our self and at one with all that is.

Being at one begins within one's self. This is not merely some theoretical concept. It can be an existential reality. We recognize it by the peace we experience when we are no longer at war with our self, no longer of two (or more) minds on matters, no longer living with a divided heart. Søren Kierkegaard called it purity of heart and described it as the ability to will one thing. It is a singularity that, when experienced, rings true with the sound of a bell that has no cracks threatening to fragment it.

But being at one with our own self can only happen when we are at one with life, with the world, and with all that is. This only comes after we have raised the white flag of surrender in our war with life—when we stop demanding that it come to us on our terms and resisting it whenever it proves obstinate in submitting to our control. Peace within our self is a precondition to peace with others and with life.

I do not believe that any of this can happen without spirituality. Our relationship to that which is beyond the self makes these transformations within the depths of our selves possible. It is our relationship to the self-transcendent that allows us to be fully alive in the present and fully present to our selves and to others in that moment. A life lived soulfully and spiritually is a life that can support the human development that is involved in becoming fully human. Practices of soulful spirituality keep us grounded in our bodies while supporting us as we reach out beyond them to embrace life and all that is. They connect us to our depths and leave us open to our heights.

Becoming at one within our selves and in relation to life and the world is a journey of willing response to the deep stirring of the Spirit within our own spirit. It does require our attention and our participation—all becoming does. It needs our cooperation. Becoming at one within our selves requires our consent to the gentle beckoning of life. It involves letting go of everything that keeps us apart from love. It is the great adventure and deep joy of becoming fully human.

I began the book with a poem by Rilke, and so it seems fitting to end with one more stanza from this profoundly soulful and spiritual young man who speaks to us from a century ago. Listen to his words and, if you dare, take his advice.

> You are not dead yet, it's not too late
> to open your depths by plunging into them
> and drink in the life
> that reveals itself quietly there.[1]

Acknowledgments

My most important learning about the matters discussed in this book has come from dialogue with people about their journeys. Much of this has occurred within my practice of psychotherapy and, in recent years, my work in spiritual guidance. To the many individuals with whom I have journeyed in these contexts I give my most profound thanks. My work with you gave me a privileged place to learn about soulful spirituality, matters not simply reflected in this book but also reflected, more importantly, in my life.

But my dialogue about the inner life has not been restricted to professional practice. I have also long been keenly interested in hearing the stories of people who are open to telling me about their attempts to live spiritually and soulfully. This has always been particularly instructive when it has allowed me to learn from people whose spiritual path has not been the same as my own. Time spent in Asia provided me with the opportunity for dialogue with Buddhists, Taoists, and followers of traditional Chinese religions. This dialogue has complemented my work in North America and Europe, which has exposed me more to Jews, Muslims, and Hindus. In Canada, this dialogue has increasingly involved people who often do not think of themselves as spiritual (and definitely do not consider themselves to be religious) but who are sufficiently committed to living with authenticity and presence that they have eagerly engaged with me in conversation around the issues discussed in this book. The dialogue I have been privileged to share in these contexts has been one of the most valuable gifts I have ever received.

A number of people and organizations deserve special mention as I acknowledge my reliance on learning through dialogue. I am particularly thankful to Dr. Ekman Tam for the opportunity to spend several extended periods of time at Tao Fong Shan Centre for Spirituality and Interfaith Dialogue in Hong Kong. I also thank the many friends I met through Areopagos, the Scandinavian organization active in fostering interfaith dialogue. In particular, I acknowledge Ole Skjerbaek Madsen, Bent Reidar Erikson, Knut Grønvik, Inger Dahl Jensen, and Lars Mollerup-Degn. I am also very thankful for the opportunity to have worked on several occasions with the staff at Modum Bad Klinikken Psyckiatrisk, a center for residential psychotherapy in Norway that provides balanced care to body, spirit, and soul. Special thanks to Dr. Berit Okkenhaug and Dr. Gunnar Fagerli for this opportunity. I am also deeply thankful to Dr. Notto R. Thelle of the University of Oslo, who gave me great help in learning from the major Asian religions.

I also wish to thank Carey Theological College (University of British Columbia, Vancouver, Canada) for their support and hospitality during the early stages of research for this book. In particular, I wish to thank Cam Yates, who facilitated my Distinguished Author in Residence appointment there. I also express my appreciation for my faculty colleagues and students at Psychological Studies Institute at Richmont Graduate University in Atlanta, where many of these ideas were first presented. I am also appreciative of the support I have received from the Centre for Studies in Religion and Society at the University of Victoria in Canada, and in particular from Dr. Michael Hadley, who introduced me to the center, and Dr. Paul Bramadat, who invited me to join them as an associate fellow. I also thank Monica Bestawros, Brian Crump, Diane Ashlock, Chris Wheelus, and Dr. Zoila Carrandang for research assistance. I am also deeply appreciative of the contributions to my understanding of the matters discussed in this book made by my friend and colleague Dr. Jackie Stinton. Regular long walks along the coast of Vancouver Island with Dr. Mark Muldoon also played a very significant role in shaping my understanding of soulful spirituality, and I thank him for the gift of his friendship.

I am also pleased to be able to acknowledge a few of the others who, over the years, have journeyed with me in friendships that have helped me cultivate my own soulful spirituality: Ed Plantinga, David and Bonne Sigston, Dr. Brenda Stephenson, Pui Fong Wong, Dr. Don

Woodside, Rabbi Emily Brenner, Dr. Irene Alexander, Father Basil Pennington, Fatima Zohra Temsamani, and Jaouad Benjelloun. Likewise, I am happy to acknowledge and thank my agent, Kathryn Helmer, for her conceptual help in the early stages of this project and for her patience and persistence in finding me such a suitable publisher. Thanks also to my editors, Bob Hosack and Arika Theule-Van Dam, for their support of this project and able assistance in bringing it to print.

Most especially, I want to thank Juliet—my wife, my soul mate, and my closest spiritual friend for four decades.

Notes

Preface

1. George Lakoff and Mark Johnson, *Metaphors We Live By* (Chicago: University of Chicago Press, 2003).

Chapter 1 The Struggle to Be Fully Alive

1. Father Basil Pennington, personal communication, October 7, 2004.

Chapter 2 Our Restless Hearts

1. Quoted in Ronald Rolheiser, *The Holy Longing: The Search for a Christian Spirituality* (New York: Doubleday, 1999), 3.

2. Idries Shah, *The Pleasantries of the Incredible Mulla Nasrudin* (London: Octagon, 1983), 93.

3. Augustine, *Basic Writings of Saint Augustine*, ed. and trans. Whitney J. Oates (Grand Rapids: Baker Books, 1980), 1:3.

4. Rolheiser, *Holy Longing*, 9.

5. These terms are far from my own, although the way I will use them will be different from how they are often used. The first two, ego inflation and deflation, are Jungian concepts that, in their technical sense, are reasonably close to the slightly broader meaning I am attaching to these words. While the concept of integration plays an important role in Jung, he means by it something different from what I mean in this chapter.

6. See, for example, the work of the New Age spiritual philosopher David Spangler, *Incarnational Spirituality* (Everett, WA: Lorian, 2008).

7. Thich Nhat Hanh, *Living Buddha, Living Christ* (New York: Riverhead Books, 1995), 7.

Chapter 3 Understanding Our Humanity

1. T. S. Eliot, "The Rock," in *The Complete Poems and Plays, 1909–1962* (New York: Harcourt Brace Jovanovich, 1991), 161.

2. *Holy Qur'an*, trans. M. H. Shakir (Elmhurst, NY: Tahrike Tarsile Qur'an, 1982), 15:26.

3. Eva Wong, trans., *Cultivating Stillness: A Taoist Manual for Transforming Body and Mind* (Boston: Shambhala, 1992), 35.

4. Thomas Moore, *The Soul's Religion: Cultivating a Profoundly Spiritual Way of Life* (New York: HarperCollins, 2002), 13.

5. There are also, of course, essential physical ingredients in the recipe for full-orbed human functioning—such things as adequate diet, exercise, and freedom from environmental toxins. However, since my focus is the development of the inner person, it is the nonmaterial aspects of the journey that will most concern us here.

6. James Legge, trans., *Li Chi: Book of Rites, Part 2* (Whitefish, MT: Kessinger, 2003).

7. See, for example, Ken Wilber, *Integral Psychology* (Boston: Shambhala, 2000) and *Integral Spirituality* (Boston: Integral Books, 2007).

8. Jean Vanier, *Becoming Human* (Toronto: House of Anansi, 2003), 1.

Chapter 4 Living with Spirit and Soul

1. Gilbert Ryle, *The Concept of Mind* (Chicago: University of Chicago Press, 1984).

2. James Hillman, *Re-Visioning Psychology* (New York: Harper & Row, 1975), x.

3. Jacques Lacan, "A Love Letter," in *Feminine Sexuality: Jacques Lacan and the École Freudienne*, ed. J. Mitchell and J. Rose (New York: Norton, 1985), 155.

4. Hillman, *Re-Visioning Psychology*, 3–50.

5. Quoted in James Hillman, *Puer Papers* (Dallas: Spring Publications, 1979), 58.

6. Thomas Moore, *The Soul's Religion: Cultivating a Profoundly Spiritual Way of Life* (New York: HarperCollins, 2002), 68.

7. Dag Hammarskjöld, *Markings* (Toronto: Random House, 1964), 19.

8. Byram Karasu, "Spiritual Psychotherapy," *American Journal of Psychotherapy*, Spring 1999, 143–62. See also Karasu, *The Art of Serenity* (New York: Simon & Schuster, 2003).

9. John O'Donohue, *Eternal Echoes: Celtic Reflections on Our Yearning to Belong* (New York: First Cliff Street Books, 1999), 2.

10. Ibid., xxvii.

Chapter 5 The Spiritual Nature of the Human Journey

1. E. H. Erikson, *Insight and Responsibility* (New York: Norton, 1964), 118.

2. David G. Benner, *The Gift of Being Yourself: The Sacred Call to Self-Discovery* (Downers Grove, IL: InterVarsity, 2004).

3. John Sanford, ed., *Fritz Kunkel: Selected Writings* (New York: Paulist, 1984), 66.

4. Here, and in most instances that follow, I use "mother" to mean the primary caretaker.

5. Margaret Mahler, Fred Pine, and Anni Bergman, *The Psychological Birth of the Human Infant* (New York: Basic Books, 1975).

6. Sanford, *Fritz Kunkel*, 29.

7. James Hollis, *The Middle Passage: From Misery to Meaning in Midlife* (Toronto: Inner City Books, 1993), 41.

8. C. G. Jung, *Letters* (Princeton: Princeton University Press, 1975), 2:265.

Chapter 6 Deep Religion and Healthy Spirituality

1. William James, *The Varieties of Religious Experience* (New York: Touchstone, 1997), 485–86.

2. Thomas Moore, *The Soul's Religion: Cultivating a Profoundly Spiritual Way of Life* (New York: HarperCollins, 2002), 268.

3. Khalifa Abdul Hakim, *The Prophet and His Message* (Lahore, Pakistan: The Institute of Islamic Culture, 1972), 322.

4. Quoted in Morris Berman, *Coming to Our Senses: Body and Spirit in the Hidden History of the West* (New York: Simon & Schuster, 1989), 41.

5. Moore, *Soul's Religion*, 46.

6. Dean Ornish, "Love as Though Your Very Survival Depended on It," in *Healing the Heart of the World*, ed. Dawson Church (Santa Rosa, CA: Elite Books, 2005), 311.

Chapter 7 Embodied Spirituality

1. Sigmund Freud, *The Ego and the Id* (New York: Norton, 1990).

2. James Nelson, *The Intimate Connection: Male Sexuality, Masculine Spirituality* (Louisville: Westminster John Knox, 1988), 68–69.

3. Marvin Ellison, "Refusing to Be a Good Soldier," in *Redefining Sexual Ethics*, ed. Susan Davies and Eleanor Haney (Cleveland: Pilgrim Press, 1991), 435.

4. Morris Berman, *Coming to Our Senses: Body and Spirit in the Hidden History of the West* (New York: Simon & Schuster, 1989), 36.

5. Recent neuropsychological research disputes the popular notion that emotions are the enemy of rationality. In fact, emotions are vital to higher cognitive functioning and are actually essential to good judgment. Antonio Damasio, in his book *The Feeling of What Happens: Body, Emotion and the Making of Consciousness* (London: Heinemann, 1999), presents his research demonstrating that while people with brain damage that affects emotional regulation may be able to perform to a high level on most intelligence tests, they display gross defects of planning, judgment, and social appropriateness. These defects are caused by their inability to respond emotionally to the content of their thoughts. Evidently, unlike oil and water, emotions and reason do mix quite well together. In fact, decisions that are informed by both may well be the best.

6. Ronald Rolheiser, *The Holy Longing: The Search for a Christian Spirituality* (New York: Doubleday, 1999), 194.

7. In talking about the way body, spirit, and soul contribute to sexuality, I will be drawing on and adapting insights from the very helpful work of Daniel Helminiak, *The Human Core of Spirituality: Mind as Psyche and Spirit* (Albany: State University of New York Press, 1996).

8. Ibid., 249.

9. Ibid., 243.

10. Quoted in Rolheiser, *Holy Longing*, 204.

11. I am thankful to my colleague Jackie Stinton for this important insight.

12. Thomas Moore, *The Soul's Religion: Cultivating a Profoundly Spiritual Way of Life* (New York: HarperCollins, 2002), 140.

13. Paul Ricoeur, "Wonder, Eroticism and Enigma," in *Sexuality and Identity*, ed. Hendrik Ruitenbeek (New York: Dell, 1970), 13–22.

14. Ann and Barry Ulinov, *The Healing Imagination: The Meeting of Psyche and Soul* (Einsiedein: Daimon Verlag, 2000), 76.

15. Daniel Ladinsky, *I Heard God Laughing: Poems of Hope and Joy; Renderings of Hafiz* (New York: Penguin Books, 2006). Copyright 1996 and 2006 by Daniel Ladinsky and used with his permission.

16. Teilhard de Chardin, *Science and Christ* (New York: Harper & Row, 1968), 12.

Chapter 8 Awareness

1. Ken McCloud, *Wake to Your Life: Discovering the Buddhist Path of Attention* (New York: HarperOne, 2002).

2. Joseph Goldstein and Jack Kornfield, *Seeking the Heart of Wisdom: The Path of Insight Meditation* (Boston: Shambhala, 2001), 3.

3. Pir Vilayat Inayat Khan, *Awakening: A Sufi Experience* (New York: Tarcher, 2000).

4. Mary Oliver, "Low Tide," *Amicus Journal*, Winter 2001, 34.

5. G. I. Gurdjieff, *Beelzebub's Tales to His Grandson*, All and Everything, 1st ser. (New York: Penguin, 1964).

6. Simone Weil, *Waiting for God*, trans. Emma Craufurd (San Francisco: Harper & Row, 1951), 111.

7. Simone Weil, *Gravity and Grace*, trans. Emma Craufurd (New York: Routledge & Kegan Paul, 1987), 106.

8. Douglas Steere, *Prayer in the Contemporary World* (Wallingford, PA: Pendle Hill Publications, 1990), 4.

9. Saint Benedict, *The Rule of St. Benedict in English*, ed. Timothy Fry (New York: Vintage Books, 1998), 1.

10. Eckhart Tolle, *A New Earth: Awakening to Your Life's Purpose* (New York: Plume, 2005), 115.

11. Daniel J. Siegel, *The Mindful Brain: Reflection and Attunement in the Cultivation of Well-Being* (New York: Norton, 2007).

12. Ibid., 172.

13. Cynthia Bourgeault, *Centering Prayer and Inner Awakening* (Cambridge, MA: Cowley, 2004), 13.

14. C. G. Jung, *Letters of C. G. Jung*, vol. 1, *1906–1950* (London: Routledge, 1973), 377.

15. A number of other very helpful suggestions about how to learn to pay attention, with particular treatment of how these fit within Christian spirituality, can be found in Leighton Ford, *The Attentive Life: Discerning God's Presence in All Things* (Downers Grove, IL: InterVarsity, 2008).

Chapter 9 Wonder

1. William Wordsworth, *The Complete Poetical Works of William Wordsworth* (Whitefish, MT: Kessinger Publishing, 2006), 1:403.

2. Albert Einstein, *Ideas and Opinions*, trans. Sonja Bargmann (New York: Bonanza Books, 1988), 11.

3. Elizabeth Barrett Browning, *Aurora Leigh* (Oxford: Oxford University Press, 1998), 265.

4. *The Gift: Poems by Hafiz*, trans. Daniel Ladinsky (New York: Penguin, 1999). Copyright 1999 by Daniel Ladinsky and used with his permission.

5. Einstein, *Ideas and Opinions*, 11.

6. Abraham Joshua Heschel, *Man Is Not Alone: A Philosophy of Religion* (New York: Farrar, Straus and Young, 1951).

7. Ibid., 13.

8. William Wordsworth, "Lines Composed a Few Miles above Tintern Abbey," in *Poems* (New York: Everyman's Library, 1995), 50.

9. John O'Donohue, *Eternal Echoes: Celtic Reflections on Our Yearning to Belong* (New York: First Cliff Street Books, 1999), 198.

10. Jhumpa Lahiri, *Interpreter of Maladies: Stories* (Boston: Houghton Mifflin, 1999), 198.

11. Eugene Peterson, *Christ Plays in Ten Thousand Places* (Grand Rapids: Eerdmans, 2005), 123.

12. Matthew Fox, *Creation Spirituality: Liberating Gifts for the Peoples of the Earth* (San Francisco: HarperSanFrancisco, 1991).

Chapter 10 Otherness

1. Margaret Silf, *Inner Compass: An Invitation to Ignatian Spirituality* (Chicago: Loyola Press, 1999), xiii.

2. Emmanuel Levinas, *Totality and Infinity: An Essay on Exteriority*, trans. A. Lingus (Pittsburgh: Duquesne University Press, 1969), 73.

3. Melanie Klein, *Envy and Gratitude, and Other Works, 1946–1963* (London: Hogarth, 1984).

4. Anthony Storr, *Feet of Clay: A Study of Gurus* (London and New York: HarperCollins, 1997), 160.

5. Saint Benedict, *The Rule of St. Benedict in English*, ed. Timothy Fry (New York: Vintage Books, 1998), 51.

6. Martin Buber, *I and Thou*, trans. W. Kaufmann (New York: Free Press, 1971).

7. James L. Fredricks, "Interreligious Friendship: A New Theological Virtue," *Journal of Ecumenical Studies* 35 (1998): 159–74.

8. Thich Nhat Hanh, *Living Buddha, Living Christ* (New York: Riverhead Books, 1995), 9.

9. Jeffrey Bloechl, ed., *The Face of the Other and the Trace of God: Essays on the Philosophy of Emmanuel Levinas* (New York: Fordham University Press, 2000).

10. Richard Norris, *Understanding the Faith of the Church* (New York: Seabury, 1979), 76.

11. Rudolf Otto, *The Idea of the Holy*, trans. John W. Harvey (New York: Oxford University Press, 1958).

12. The Hebrew name for God is YHWH, often referred to as the sacred tetragrammaton and translated by Christians as *Yahweh*. Composed of the four Hebrew letters *yod*, *he*, *waw*, and *he*, the name YHWH was an unspeakable word for Jews.

Richard Rohr suggests that the correct pronunciation of YHWH may well have been an attempt to replicate and imitate the sound of breathing (*The Naked Now: Learning to See as the Mystics See* [New York: Crossroad Publishing, 2009], 25). The one thing we do every moment of our lives is therefore to speak the name of God, this being our first and our last word as we enter and leave the world. This helps us understand why attentiveness to breathing is such an important spiritual practice and why it is so congruent with Christian spirituality.

13. Buber, *I and Thou.*

14. Carl Rogers, *On Becoming a Person: A Therapist's View of Psychotherapy* (New York: Mariner Books, 1995).

15. James Mundackal, *Man in Dialogue* (Alwaye, India: Pontifical Institute Publications, 1977), 103–4.

Chapter 11 Reality

1. Thomas Merton, *Thoughts in Solitude* (Boston: Shambhala, 1993), 3.

2. Jelaluddin Rumi, *Selected Poems: Rumi*, trans. Coleman Barks (Baltimore: Penguin, 2004), 109. Copyright © Coleman Barks, 1995. Reproduced by permission of Penguin Books Ltd.

3. Richard Rohr, *Things Hidden: Scripture as Spirituality* (Cincinnati: St. Anthony Messenger, 2008), 126.

4. Adapted from an apocryphal story that can be found in many places, including Miriyam Glazer, ed., *Dancing on the Edge of the World: Jewish Stories of Faith, Inspiration, and Love* (Chicago: Lowell House, 2000), 31.

5. See David G. Benner, *The Gift of Being Yourself: The Sacred Call to Self-Discovery* (Downers Grove, IL: InterVarsity, 2004) for a fuller discussion of the importance of knowing and being our self in Christian spirituality.

6. Thomas Moore, *The Soul's Religion: Cultivating a Profoundly Spiritual Way of Life* (New York: HarperCollins, 2002), 89.

7. Quoted in John Howard Griffin, *Follow the Ecstasy* (Fort Worth: Latitude, 1983), 104.

8. Florida Scott Maxwell, *The Measure of My Days* (New York: Penguin Books, 1983), 42.

9. Thomas Merton, *New Seeds of Contemplation* (New York: New Directions, 1961).

Chapter 12 Presence

1. James E. Loder, *The Transforming Moment*, 2nd ed. (Colorado Springs: Helmers & Howard, 1989), 70.

2. Sigmund Freud, *Three Essays on the Theory of Sexuality* (New York: Basic Books, 1962), 90n1.

3. Eva Wong, trans., *Cultivating Stillness: A Taoist Manual for Transforming Body and Mind* (Boston: Shambhala, 1992), 41–44.

4. John O'Donohue, *Anam Cara: A Book of Celtic Wisdom* (New York: HarperCollins, 1977), 16.

5. I said that while meditation and prayer share important features they are not the same. However, Centering Prayer is a form of Christian meditation that is practiced

not for its psychospiritual benefits but as prayer. It is a way of opening oneself to God and being with God. I will have more to say about it shortly.

6. Jill Price, *The Woman Who Can't Forget: The Extraordinary Story of Living with the Most Remarkable Memory Known to Science; A Memoir* (New York: Free Press, 2008).

7. This is, of course, a very oversimplified presentation of Centering Prayer. For fuller treatment, see M. Basil Pennington, OCSO, *Centering Prayer: Renewing an Ancient Christian Prayer Form* (New York: Image Books, 2001).

8. Richard Rohr, *The Naked Now: Learning to See as the Mystics See* (New York: Crossroad Publishing, 2009), 60.

Chapter 13 Surrender

1. Dag Hammarskjöld, *Markings* (Toronto: Random House, 1964), 180.

2. Ruth Penny, personal communication, September 17, 2008. ⟶⧸⟵

3. Developed by Mary Mrozowski as a way to move Centering Prayer from a meditative practice into active life, Welcoming Prayer is described in Cynthia Bourgeault, *Centering Prayer and Inner Awakening* (Cambridge, MA: Cowley, 2004), 135–52.

4. Donald Trump, "My #1 Tip for Living Large," *Money Sense*, December/January 2007, 5.

5. Bourgeault, *Centering Prayer*, 84.

Epilogue

1. "Du siehst, ich viel . . . /You see, I want a . . . ," in *Rilke's Book of Hours: Love Poems to God* by Rainer Maria Rilke, trans. Anita Barrows and Joanna Macy (New York: Riverhead Books, 1996). Copyright © 1996 by Anita Barrows and Joanna Macy. Used by permission of Riverhead Books, an imprint of Penguin Group (USA) Inc.

Index